Making & Keeping
CREATIVE
JOURNALS

Making & Keeping
CREATIVE
JOURNALS

Suzanne J. E. Tourtillott

LARK BOOKS

A Division of Sterling Publishing Company, Inc.
NEW YORK

EDITOR:
Suzanne J. E. Tourtillott

ASSISTANT EDITORS:
Veronika Alice Gunter
Heather Smith

ART DIRECTOR:
Susan McBride
Kathy Holmes

PHOTOGRAPHY:
Evan Bracken

ILLUSTRATIONS:
Wendy Simons

Library of Congress Cataloging-in-Publication Data

Available

10 9 8 7 6 5 4 3 2 1

Published by Lark Books, a division of
Sterling Publishing Co., Inc.
387 Park Avenue South, New York, N.Y. 10016

From *Envisioning Information* by Edward R. Tufte. Copyright @ 1997
by Edward R. Tufte. All rights reserved. Reprinted by permission of
Graphics Press.
From *The Diary of Anais Nin*, 1947-1955. Copyright @ 1974 by Anais
Nin. All rights reserved. Reprinted by permission of Harcourt, Inc.,
and Author's Representative, Gunther Stuhlman.

Distributed in Canada by Sterling Publishing,
c/o Canadian Manda Group, One Atlantic Ave., Suite 105
Toronto, Ontario, Canada M6K 3E7

Distributed in the U.K. by:
Guild of Master Craftsman Publications Ltd.
Castle Place
166 High Street
Lewes
East Sussex
England
BN7 1XU
Tel: (+ 44) 1273 477374
Fax: (+ 44) 1273 478606
Email: pubs@thegmcgroup.com
Web: www.gmcpublications.com

Distributed in Australia by Capricorn Link (Australia) Pty Ltd., P.O.
Box 6651,
Baulkham Hills, Business Centre
NSW 2153, Australia

If you have questions or comments about this book, please contact:
Lark Books
50 College St.
Asheville, NC 28801
(828) 253-0467

Manufactured in Hong Kong by Dai Nippon

ISBN 1-57990-214-6

For my mother, Suzanne Montgomery, who, by her own example, taught me to love books.

CONTENTS

Jaunt; 1999; Elizabeth Clark, *Mussaku*, Phoenix, Ariz.; 6 $\frac{1}{2}$ x 5 x $\frac{7}{8}$ inches
(16.5 x 12.7 x 2.2 cm); simplified binding; photo by John Morrow

INTRODUCTION

"A poem, a sentence, causes us to be ourselves. I be and I see my being at the same time."
—Ralph Waldo Emerson

This book will introduce you to two fascinating and rewarding activities: the practice of journal keeping and the craft of making books. Both these creative endeavors—writing and craft—are time-honored pursuits that can reward and enrich your daily life. We hope to show you that a custom journal made by your own hand can be a companionable witness to your love of words and books. Within these covers you'll find helpful information, and perhaps inspiration, about each of them.

To begin, we'll briefly explore some of the reasons why so many of us feel compelled to put pen to paper, to dialogue with ourselves, and to record our thoughts and experiences. We'll also look at ways to motivate your writing impulse; these tried and true methods are designed to stimulate the writer within you.

Book making, like journaling, can also result in tangible personal benefits and satisfying, creative expression. The projects included in this book show you the work of five talented book artists who agreed to collaborate with 13 journalers, to create unique journal designs that suit the journaler's individual needs. Whether the journal traveled Italy in a jacket pocket, or rested comfortably in the sunshine on a gardener's knees, each of these books was made to help the journaler chronicle life to its fullest capacity. And if you like to embellish your pages with line and color, you'll see some great examples of visual-verbal journaling here.

A beautiful handmade journal can help you perceive your inner vision in new and exciting ways. You may derive a new satisfaction and deeper commitment to your own journaling by making one or more of the projects in this book. Once you actually craft a unique creative journal, it becomes more than a mere object to write in—it can itself become a catalyst for greater awareness and movement in other areas of your life. You might even keep several journals, to reflect a life of varied interests and activities.

If you enjoy expressing your thoughts and ideas in a journal, whether in longhand or in pictures, why not do it in a special volume designed to encourage your journaling to flow more smoothly, more creatively—your place to dream, seek, express, and explore?

The Art of
JOURNAL WRITING

WHY JOURNAL?

Your journal can begin with a purpose—to study the self, address life issues, or chronicle the times. More importantly, when you make a personal investment in journaling it's bound to reward you unexpectedly, no matter what your initial reasons were for the undertaking. Journaling is serious fun: gratifying, surprising, and richly rewarding.

Not everyone has the same reasons for journaling.

Indeed, you don't need to have a "good" reason at all;

many take the view that life—and journaling—is all about being on the journey, not arriving at a destination. Let's look first at some of the reasons why people keep journals.

pages 36-37 from the journal *Pressure Points*; 1995; Wendy Hale Davis; page size 8½ x 11 inches (21.6 x 27.9 cm); pen, ink, pastepaper, photo, ticket stub; surface decoration of leather onlay and pastepaper binding; photo by Bob Daemmrich

Benefits of Journaling

I want, by understanding myself, to understand others. I want to be all that I am capable of becoming…This all sounds very strenuous and serious. But now that I have wrestled with it, it's no longer so. I feel happy—deep down. All is well.

Journal [1922], last entry.
—Katherine Mansfield

The benefit of keeping a journal is that you allow yourself pause: slowing life down to the pace of your own thoughts and words, as you put them in a medium in which you can take stock, explore, make sense of, or savor.

Journaling can also be a process by which we heal mentally and physically. Holistic educator and author Lois Guarino says that purposeful journal writing helps you find your authentic self, the person composed of your most reliable instincts, truthful insights, trustworthy observations, and genuine feelings. It's well documented that those who use journaling in order to make sense of difficult events and emotions rank higher in tests for feelings of psychological well-being—it even benefits blood-pressure readings.

Keeping a creative journal requires no special talent. In this arena of personal exploration, doubt may creep in, but don't allow it to become the one thing that keeps you from trying it. Indeed, the process of making the journal itself can be a quiet meditation, a time for the focused attention that fosters inner awareness.

pages 70-71 from the journal *Transformer;* 1993; Wendy Hale Davis; page size 8½ x 11 inches (21.6 x 27.9 cm); pen, ink, halftones, stamp; surface decoration of plain canvas; photo by Bob Daemmrich

To Record a Journey, External or Internal

The soul of a journey is liberty, perfect liberty, to think, feel, do just as one pleases. —William Hazlitt

Marco Polo, an inspiration to travelers everywhere, began his journal when he journeyed from Italy to the Far East. Following the invention of the printing press in the 15th century, Polo's 1298 book, *The Travels of Marco Polo*, was second in circulation only to the Bible. Author and philosopher C.S. Lewis traced a different kind of journey in the diary he kept from 1922 to 1927—his internal transformation from optimistic Oxford University student to lauded scholar.

Your travels may take you no farther than a solitary visit to a coffee shop or a museum, but you can write for the pleasure of documenting your surroundings. Take note of your own observations about a scene as it unfolds before you. The fact that we are someplace new and different often helps us to see—and write—with fresh eyes.

For Healing and Insight

Life can only be understood backwards; but it must be lived forwards. —Sören Kierkegaard

Exploring an event through writing, without holding back or having your thoughts derailed by those of others, can enable you to reach a level of insight needed to move forward or to make a necessary decision.

Etty Hillseum began her diary two years before her death at Auschwitz in 1943. At first, she used the diary to contemplate her intellectual pursuits and romantic affairs, but it's in her writing that Hillseum achieved spiritual growth, as she ultimately decided to forsake safe passage out of Europe to be with fellow Jews.

Repository July-Sept. 1997; Pamela Lyle Westhaven; 7½ x 6½ x 3 inches (19 x 16.5 x 7.5 cm); pages: handmade papers of wood pulp and flower blossoms; ribbon; cover: mill board, book linen, handmade papers constructed with a fore-edge flap; photo by artist

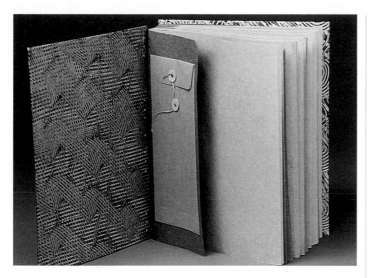

Collector's Journal; 2000; Claudia Lee; 12¼ x 9½ x 2½ inches
(31.1 x 24.1 x 6.4 cm); handmade and decorative papers,
Coptic binding with spacers, envelope pocket; photo by John Lucas

The Confessional Journal

*I never travel without my diary. One should always have something
sensational to read on the train.* —Oscar Wilde

Writer Thomas Mallon, in *A Book of One's Own*, says that
the confessional journal is motivated by a secrecy — even a
conspiracy — well symbolized by the locking diaries of many
youths. The entries in a confessional journal are often
deeply self-revealing and can have an unburdening effect.
The poet Byron called his journal a "relief."

   The journal might be a place to safely examine our own
shortcomings, if we are so inclined. Preachers and prisoners
alike have found some solace in writing about their moral
failings to that most silent of all confessors, the personal
diary.

As a Chronicle to Future Generations

There is a history in all men's lives. —William Shakespeare

Whether you pass your journal on to a younger family
member or a historical society, the joys and disappoint-
ments of a seemingly ordinary life can become interesting
and valuable reading at a later date. The personal journal
has often served as an excellent research tool for histori-

ans. Women's diaries and letters have contributed much to
our understanding of others' lives. Martha Ballard, a mid-
wife in Colonial America, dutifully made daily entries in
her journal for 27 years: "A Snow Storm & very Cold. I
have been at home ys Day. mr French informd me of ye
Death of mrs Stuart who Deceast ys morn. mr Hinkley &
Lady went past here on yr way home. I finished Ephes
Stockins & fixt Cyruss footing." The accumulation of thou-
sands of entries such as this one describes daily life in a
way that is rarely captured in traditional history books.

Nostradamus-The End of the Century Scrapbook; 1999; Ksenia
Kopystynska; 20.5 x 14¼ x 3 inches (52 x 36 x 7.5 cm); leather
(cowhide) and handmade paper, deckle edges, antique leather, etching;
photo by Contanasiuk

To Live More Fully

There is a fullness of all things, even of sleep and of love. —Homer

Illness and other confinements may limit our physical activities, but journaling can set the mind free. Anne Frank's teenage journal is an example of how writing can be a powerful element that helps us live life to its fullest, no matter what the circumstances. Frank received the diary on her 13th birthday, shortly before she and her family went into hiding in Amsterdam. She candidly chronicled more than two years of life in cramped conditions with her parents, sister, and another family. Her diary stands as a testament, not only to one girl's experience of adolescence, but as a forceful representation of human suffering in wartime.

As a Catalyst for Creative Expression

The music in my heart
I bore Long after it was
heard no more.
—William Wordsworth

Keeping a journal is, at its most fundamental level, a creative endeavor. Many writers stick strictly to the written word, but others are compelled to add pictorial elements to their pages—and images speak volumes. Emotions, memories, and messages can be meaningfully expressed by combining words with pattern and color, and much insight can spring from these simple beginnings.

Artists' journals sometimes look more like messy sketchbooks, but you can take inspiration from their lively, experimental approach to the journaling process. Image entries in a journal might take the form of scribbling, drawing, or collage that is

comprised of bits of ephemera from a life well lived—creative celebrations in ink or paint. You decide if you want your expressive, creative journal to stimulate other artistic interests, or whether it becomes a work of art itself.

When all's said and done, why you journal—and what form the journal takes—is not nearly as important as actually undertaking the process itself. The reason may be obscure or perhaps quite purposeful, but it bears repeating that the creative effort you make is its own greatest reward. You will find yourself getting better at journaling with practice—in fact, focused writing is sure to have a cumulative effect as it sharpens your senses and reveals new insights.

Being Verbal When You Write

"Writing a journal means that facing your ocean you are
afraid to swim across it, so you attempt to drink it drop by drop."
—George Sand

Penland Sketchbook; 1993; Andrea A. Peterson; 14 x 20 x 4 inches (35.6 x 50.8 x 10.2 cm); HMP, mica, washer, pastels, ink; photo by artist

A journal is bound to be full of words. But you may arrange the words any way you wish, and this opens up avenues of self-understanding you may not have imagined. No matter what your writing abilities are when you begin journaling, the process of creative journaling will improve them, allowing you to express and understand yourself better.

Journaling does require a commitment on your part. Try to carve out a time and a place where you can journal regularly. If you already enjoy sitting at a particular sun-drenched table in the late afternoon, then the time and the place are just waiting for you to use it. Write for the same amount of time, or the same amount of pages, every day, if you can. Try to be responsive to journaling by keeping one with you at all times—you can promptly pull it out of your pocket or backpack at those times of the day when you have a few minutes on your hands. It's a great way to get in the habit of spontaneously recording your experiences. Here is an introduction to a few of the many methods used to get started.

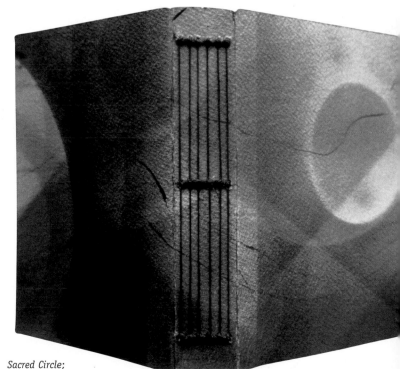

PBI 1995; 1995;
Emily Martin;
8 ½ x 7 x 2 ½ inches
(21.6 x 17.8 x 6.4 cm);
recloseable storage bags,
wooden pegs, found objects;
photo by Meryl Marek

Freewriting

"I write down everything, everything, everything. Otherwise, why should I write?" —Marie Bashkirtseff

For ten minutes, without stopping, write about a topic that interests you. The topic doesn't have to be profound or meaningful; think of it as a stretching exercise for the journaler inside you. You might write about how salt tastes, a scrap of conversation overheard, or the remarkable way rain strikes the ground.

List-Making

How long a time lies in one little word!
—William Shakespeare

Perhaps you tend to write in full sentences; we've all been taught that's the best way to fully express a thought. But why not challenge yourself to describe the thought in a word or two, then list all the words that come to mind about the subject? Do it quickly, without editing yourself, and you might be surprised at the results. Everything you think about putting down on paper is worthy of your time. A journal is no place to be self-conscious. Be spontaneous.

Sacred Circle;
1999, Mary Crest; 6³/₄ x 5³/₄ x 2 inches
(17.1 x 14.6 x 5.1 cm); collage, printmaking, pockets, Coptic stitch;
cover: airbrushed watercolor paper over boards; photo by artist

Narrative Description

We write to heighten our...awareness of life...
to taste life twice, in the moment and
in retrospection...”
—Anaïs Nin

Another way of using words is to write with great detail and vivid language. Even the most mundane task you've mentioned in your journal can be expanded with descriptive phrases that concentrate on the five senses: touch, taste, smell, sound, and sight. When you note the particulars and try to recognize seemingly insignificant details, you'll become more aware that these random moments actually create the texture of our lives. In this way, you train your eyes and your mind to see more clearly. And that makes for more satisfying journaling.

pages 144–145 from
the journal *Pressure Points*; 1995;
Wendy Hale Davis; page size 8½ x 11 inches
(21.6 x 27.9 cm); pen, ink, pastepaper, photo, ticket stub;
surface decoration of leather onlay and pastepaper binding;
photo by Bob Daemmrich

Collector's Journal; 2000; Claudia Lee; 12¼ x 9½ x 2½ inches
(31.1 x 24.1 x 6.4 cm); handmade and decorative papers, Coptic binding
with spacers, envelope pocket; photo by John Lucas

Dreams

"He looked at his own soul with a telescope. What seemed all irregular,
he saw and shewed to be beautiful constellations; and he
added to conciousness hidden, world within worlds."
—Samuel Coleridge

Dreams are words and pictures from the unconscious. Chronicle your dreams by writing them down as completely as you can before they slip away. The experts say to do this before you've moved around too much after waking, so keep your journal by your bedside. After you've written as much as you can, write about the dream from a particular perspective. Perhaps every person in your dream represents some aspect of yourself. Examine the most important parts of the dream using one of the many books on dream analysis.

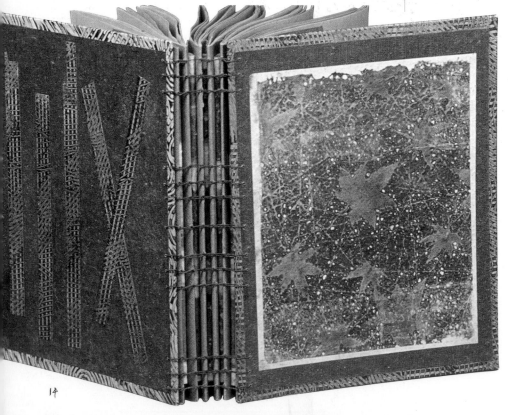

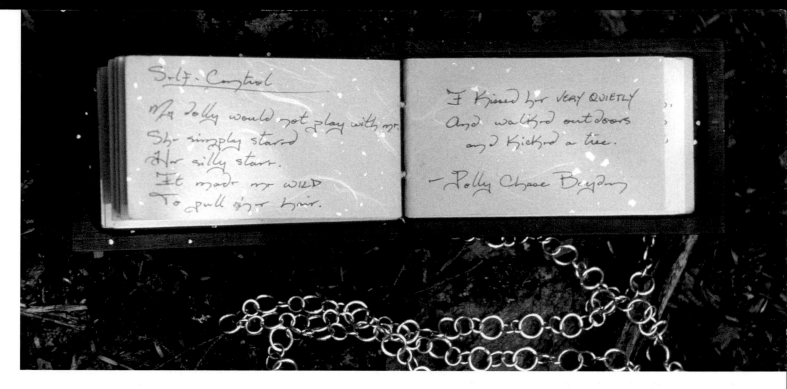

Recipes for Motherhood; 1999; Stephanie Dean-Moore;
3 x 5 x $^{13}/_{16}$ inches (7.6 x 12.5 x 2 cm); wood, sterling silver closures and
link chain to allow journal to be worn; paper, linen thread, Coptic wood
cover; surface decoration of metal piercing work, riveting; photo by artist

Poetry

*The wonderful becomes familiar and the familiar
wonderful.* —Edward R. Tufte

Look to your writing for the
seeds of a poem. Look for a
fresh turn of phrase or a
rhythm in your writing that
stands out from the rest of
the entry. Listen for the
small detail that seems to
distill some experience, and
how that particular word
seems to resonate in you.
Make a poem from a list of
words you made while free-
associating from one word to
the next.

NYC Sketchbook; 1995; Andrea A. Peterson; 10 x 16 x 2 inches
(25.4 x 40.6 x 5.1 cm); text, pastels; photo by artist

Salt Spring 2000; 2000; Pamela Lyle Westhaven; 8½ x 5½ x¾ inches (20.5 cm x 14 x 2 cm); paper: assorted papers, memorabilia, small paper bags and envelope corners hold memorabilia; surface decorations: watercolor pencils, pencil, crayons, handwritten text; photo by artist

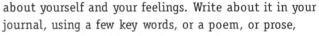

HOW TO WRITE A VISUAL JOURNAL

"Inside you there's an artist you don't know about."
—Jalal-Uddin Rumi

In order to begin a creative visual journal, all that is necessary is that you become willing to use whatever materials and thoughts are at hand for the purpose of self expression. You may use words to explore your thoughts, but a journal needn't be made of words alone. Including thoughts in visual form allows you to connect with your intuitive self. Symbols, color, and images play important roles in our lives. Pictures you draw yourself, magazine reproductions, photographs, and bits of memorabilia from daily life all qualify as visual items. The action of adding these to your journal can be a process of opening up to your emotions about the images you're using. Ask yourself what the picture tells you about yourself and your feelings. Write about it in your journal, using a few key words, or a poem, or prose, alongside the picture, right on top of it, or wherever you see fit.

Keep some favorite artistic media handy. Use colored pencils, markers, rubber stamps, paints, scissors, a glue stick. A situation you desire or fear, memories, fantasies—any of these can lend themselves to your own imaginative response or interpretation. Stick figures and scribbles are fine, and so is inaccuracy. Why inaccuracy? Because you're being true to yourself, not to other perspectives.

Your private art-making is an opportunity to connect with your unconscious feelings about yourself, others, and the world. You may begin to draw yourself much smaller or larger than those around you, or the sky much brighter or dark-

Pondering Daze; 2000; Sheila Cunningham, Richardson, Texas; 9 x 12 x 2 inches (22.9 x 30.5 x 5.1 cm); watercolor and decorative paper, envelopes, fold-in pages, pockets, grommets; cover: punched shapes with colored vellums, decorative papers, grommets; photo by artist

er than it was that day. Then you can address what you're saying with them. You're not trying to rise to any standard; you're drawing to explore and express what can't be said in words. Don't listen to that voice in your head that says, "I can't draw." No one ever has to see it but you.

Writer's Journal; 1999; Roberta Lavadour, Pendleton, Ore.; Arches cover black, German Ingres, text weight paper, found objects, memorabilia, pocket; sewn board binding; photo by artist

PERSONAL PASSIONS

Let us savor the fleeting delights of our most beautiful days! —Alphonse de Lamartine

If you have a deep connection to something that engages or intrigues you, and if you want to look more closely at how you relate to it—whether it's a quilt, a dream, or a grandchild—you have the beginnings of a creative journal inside you. Take your journal into the garden and write about the warmth of the soil. Paste the train schedule from your trip to a foreign country onto a page, then recall the sights, sounds, and smells you experienced there. Draw a picture that expresses the loss you felt when your childhood pet died. All it takes is time, energy, and a curiosity to find out more about the most fascinating subject in the world: yourself.

Bell Cow, Turning Points; 1999; Mary Crest; 6½ x 5¾ x 2 inches (16.5 x 14.6 x 5.1 cm); computer-generated and handwritten text, scanned photos, collage, printmaking, hand-marbled dividers; cover: suede; photo by artist

Ordinary Time; 2000; Mary Crest; 9 ½ x 6 ¾ x 2 inches (24.1 x 17.1 x 5.1 cm); handmade paper made with flowers and leaves; cover: covered boards with tie closure; photo by artist

A surprising number of journalers make their own journals. In the next section, you'll find lots of helpful information about what you need to get started making your very own creative journal.

The Craft of
MAKING JOURNALS

JOURNAL MATERIALS

In this book, you will find journals made with all sorts of materials—from fabric endpapers to leather and even wood covers. For the purpose of making a fine journal, you should learn a little about paper and the other basic materials that are best suited to the book arts.

About Paper

If you want your books to last a long time, use high-quality papers, and avoid those made from wood pulp, an acidic and nonarchival material. Papers that are considered *archival*, or *pH neutral*, will keep their original color and flexibility for years to come. One hundred percent cotton rag drawing and watercolor papers make great text pages; they're versatile in that you can use a variety

Fine papers

of writing and drawing media. Recycled papers may have some cotton content, but they'll also contain other, shorter fibers. Moreover, recycled paper is made from pulp that has been processed twice, and its fibers are thus often very short; the resulting paper is usually weak, tears easily, and may quickly turn brittle and yellow the way newspaper does.

Fine machine and handmade papers, on the other hand, are made from broken-down plant fibers, such as hemp, banana, cotton, or flax. Although they undergo a real beating in the papermaking process, the fibers aren't chopped into tiny pieces.

When pulped plant material is formed into sheets, the longer fibers sometimes organize themselves in a predominant direction, called *grain*, either along the length or the width of the sheet. The lack of a discernible grain pattern doesn't necessarily indicate a weak, acidic paper, though. Most handmade papers lack a dominant grain pattern but are still very durable.

It's very important that all the grained paper and board used to make a fine journal be oriented so that their grain patterns run in the same direction as the book's spine. Paper grain responds to the moisture in adhesives by swelling much more in a crosswise direction than it does with the grain, before it shrinks again as it dries. When two grain patterns cross one another (say, if the grain of a cover board and the grain of a cover paper run opposite one another), then the board and paper may pull against each other and become unglued as the adhesive dries and the materials shrink in opposing directions. If ungrained paper or material, such as book cloth or leather, is used on one side of a board while a grained paper is used on the other side, the boards will buckle. It's therefore necessary to line ungrained material with a sheet of grained paper in order to balance the pull of the grained paper on the other side of the board (see figures 1a-c). Even with nonadhesive bindings, pages turn more easily and folds are smoother and less likely to crack when their grain is aligned with the book's spine.

Finding the Grain of the Paper

It's easy to find the grain of most good paper, especially when it's still in one large sheet. Pick up one edge of the paper and bring it over, without creasing it, to meet the opposite edge. Observe the way the top of the sheet sits in relation to the bottom. Open the paper so it's flat again, then repeat the process with the other two edges (see figure 2). In the direction of the grain, the paper on top lies more nearly flat to the sheet underneath it, but when the paper is rolled against the grain, the paper curls high above the bottom sheet. You can also find the grain of paper and boards by flexing them in your hands, feeling for the resistance in the cross-grain direction. Find the grain of a small piece of paper by moistening it so that it curls; the grain will run parallel to (not across) the curl.

Once you've found the grain direction, carefully mark your paper—pencil only—with an arrow. Be sure to indicate the grain direction on cut sheets and scraps, too.

Choosing the Right Papers

Paper sellers usually refer to commercially made paper by its weight per 500 sheets, or ream. Photocopier-type *bond* paper weighs about 20 lbs. (9.1 kg), while fine paper may range from a medium weight 80 lb. (36.3 kg) sheet to an unfoldable, heavyweight 300 lbs. (136.2 kg). The terms light, medium, and heavy, describe in a general way the density and flexibility of papers without a specific weight, such as delicate Japanese tissue or other handmade papers.

Bookmakers find it useful to describe paper according to its function in the book. Before you choose your text paper, consider how you intend to use it in the journal. Most writers want a smooth, ink-friendly paper for their jotting; it's important to choose a sized paper for this. Sizing is a glue added to the paper pulp that stops ink from bleeding.

Any weight of paper may be used for the pages, but *text weight* papers are traditionally similar in weight and surface to that found in commercially bound books. At an art supply store, drawing paper, lightweight watercolor paper, and even vellum work well for writing, drawing, and pasting or collage. You might experiment with the new light-colored gel inks on rich, dark papers for text pages, the way the journaler did for the Dream Journal on page 45.

Not every page in your journal need be writerly: interleave textured, colored, heavyweight, or highly decorative papers with your text pages; they may inspire you to new creative heights. Semitransparent overlays of tracing paper, glassine, and vellum can be functional or decorative, depending on your needs; several of the journals, such as the Quilter's Journal (page 89) use them in interesting ways.

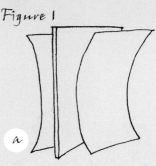

Figure 1

a

The two grained papers on either side of the cover board exert equal pull on the board as they dry.

b

The ungrained paper (such as a decorative endpaper) will buckle away from it because of the pull of the grained paper on the other side, and the board will warp.

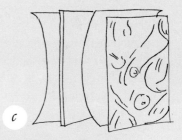

c

Use a liner of grained paper between the board and the ungrained paper.

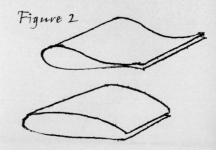

Figure 2

Choosing the Right Cover Material

The quality of your cover material is an important consideration because the cover takes a lot of wear and tear. Materials such as thin leather, fabric, and medium-weight papers are both durable and flexible. Whatever material you choose for the journal cover should be flexible enough to wrap around the edges of your boards—but look at the Yoga Journal (page 47) for an interesting alternative to gluing cover materials onto boards.

Book cloth is used for many of the journals in this book. Because it's an especially close-woven material that is backed with a special tissue or treated with a filler, adhesives won't migrate through it. There are many beautiful book cloths available—some are even made of silk! You can completely cover the boards with cloth, or combine it with a complementary decorative paper; see the combination used in the Hollow Back Spine Journal on page 113. Yard goods, such as closely woven cotton and linen, are readily available at fabric stores. Adhesives can seep through them, so you must fuse the cloth to 20-lb. (9.1 kg) paper, using an iron-on

Book cloth

fusing tissue available at fabric stores. You can spray the front with a cloth-guard spray to protect it from dirt.

Leather is available through leather-craft suppliers, but it's a good idea to use leather especially prepared for bookbinding because it's free of the the destructive acids common to the tanning and coloring processes of ordinary leather. A bookbinder's supply will have a wide selection of hides and skins. You can use heavier leathers if the corners won't be wrapped, such as for the Girdle Book (page 119) or the Travel Journal (page 39).

Book Board

Bookbinder's board is a rigid, dense, gray paperboard and can be cut with a paper trimmer. If you don't have one, you can easily cut through the board using a sharp, heavy-duty mat knife. Check for grain direction by flexing the board in both directions and feeling for the resistance. As with other paper materials, archival-quality boards are available. Other kinds of paperboard used to make covers include museum board, mat board, pasteboard, and various types of chipboard. Choose a board that is between $^1/_8$ inch (3 mm) and $^1/_{16}$ inch (1.6mm) thick, or laminate (adhere) two thinner boards together. In this book there are also several unusual journals made with thin wood boards; your choice of wood is optional for them.

Choosing the Right Adhesives

An entire chapter could be written on glues, pastes, and adhesives in general! There are several important factors to think about when choosing an adhesive: the strength of the bond, its flexibility after drying, how much it wrinkles during the drying, and its pH level. Each adhesive has its advantages and disadvantages— and some are not well suited to the stress that a well-used journal will undergo. The handy glue stick is one of these; it's better suited to light-duty jobs, such as collage. White craft glue, made of polyvinyl acetate (PVA), glides on easily, dries quickly (at times, too fast!), and bonds tightly. If PVA is left to dry in a brush, however, the brush will be ruined (see also page 24).

Book board

Adhesives in powder form

There are pH-neutral PVA glues available from bookbinder's and art and craft suppliers. Wheat paste is inexpensive and easy to make on the stove or in the microwave. It's slower drying than PVA, can be removed from almost anything (even when dry), and is not toxic or acidic. For the projects in this book, whenever you are instructed to use PVA to glue paper to paper, you can safely use either PVA or wheat paste.

Microwave Wheat Paste Adhesive

Whisk ¼ cup (28 g) of unsifted pastry or rice flour with ¼ cup (60 mL) of cold water until smooth. Bring ¾ cup (180 mL) of water to a boil in the microwave, then slowly pour the flour-water mixture into the very hot water, stirring constantly. The paste is ready to be used. If it doesn't thicken right up, put it back into the microwave for a just few seconds more. Store the paste in a marked, tightly covered container in the refrigerator. Mix a bit of acid-free PVA with wheat paste, if you want it to have greater tack and a shorter drying time.

PVA adhesive

Bookbinder's linen tape

Thread and Tape

Most of the journal pages in this book are sewn together with strong linen or cotton thread. Many of them are also supported with a woven, nonadhesive ribbon called *linen tape*, which is sewn across the spine of the text block. Sewn signatures make stronger books than glued-together single sheets (known as *perfect binding*), because the thread and tape take most of the stress of the page-turning. If you prefer, you can substitute cotton thread and draw it through a bit of beeswax. Bookbinding thread comes in lots of nice colors, so you can coordinate it with the overall design scheme of your journal.

Waxed thread

Book leather

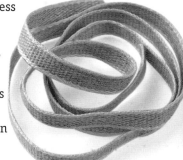

Bookbinder's linen tape

Thread

Keeping the Work and the Work Space Clean

Waste paper keeps the glue where you want it; use old phone book pages to protect your work. Moisture-resistant wax paper is perfect for wrapping just-glued parts of the book, such as the covers, before they're set aside to dry. Be sure to keep a wastebasket nearby, and throw the gluey waste paper into it right away, before it migrates onto your beautiful cover paper! If possible, cover the worktable where you do your gluing with large sheets of butcher or kraft paper, and replace them when necessary. An even simpler alternative is to do your pasting on a glass surface. It cleans up quickly, with less likelihood of accidentally setting your material on a gluey waste sheet. Have a clean, dry area for nonpasting work, too—it's all too easy to attract smudges of glue and dirt! Be sure to keep a dry and a damp rag handy for your fingers and also a jar of water for resting the glue brush in when it won't be used for a few minutes.

Once you've choosen the materials that will define the look and feel of your journal, you're almost ready to begin. The next section covers the details about tool basics.

TOOLS

The right tools help you get the best possible results. Only a few tools are needed to make your creative journal, but these are indispensable. Build your bookbinder's tool kit with these basic items, and keep them handy for every project.

Cutting Tools

Choose cutting tools that are appropriate for the material you want to cut. A craft knife is a good all-purpose tool for light- or medium-weight materials, such as paper and light board. Use a heavy-duty box cutter or mat knife to cut book board. If you use a metal-edge ruler, your cuts will be perfectly straight, and a self-healing cutting mat under your work saves wear and tear on the work surface. For cutting cloth and leather, heavy-duty scissors provide plenty of control over the material. Add scallops and zig-zags to envelope flaps and other parts of your text pages with decorative-edge scissors from a craft store.

A paper trimmer gives sharp, square cuts every time, and it can cut several pieces of paper or a single piece of board at one time. For larger cutting jobs, quick-print shops have electric cutters that can chop through dozens of pages at a time. These workhorse cutters make quick work of dense book board or a tall stack of single sheets.

Wherever possible, the projects in this book begin by listing the cut dimensions of the materials you'll be using.

Cutting tools

Bone Folder

The *bone folder* is a very useful
tool that helps you press down, or
burnish, just-glued paper and cloth.
It's usually made of bone, but there are
plastic ones, too. They come in a variety of sizes and
shapes; buy one that looks like a tongue depressor. This
seemingly simple article has many useful traits: the long
sides taper to a dull edge, perfect for folding paper. In
some designs, one end may be pointed, useful for tucking
into tight spots and also for scoring fold lines. The blunt-
ly rounded end is used for burnishing and may have a slightly convex surface on one side of the blunt end and a con-
cave surface on the other. Change the shape of a bone
folder by sanding it to suit your individual needs.

Bone folders

Tools for Making Holes

Text pages are joined by sewing, but it's not the sewing
needle that makes the holes. Instead, use a pointed hand
tool called an *awl* (or *needle awl* or *bradawl*) to pierce or
drill the sewing holes in your signatures. A clay pin tool
makes an excellent awl. A special V-shaped trough, or cradle, is used by the pros to help them hold the signature
while making the holes; turn to Preparing Signatures for
Sewing, page 26, for an easy alternative.

A *stitching awl* is a hand tool that sews through stiff
fabric and leather in one motion; a bobbin on the awl
holds the waxed thread, like a sewing machine. This tool
is perfect for the type of stitching used in the Yoga
Journal, on page 47, but the designer says you
can use a sewing machine instead. A standard office three-hole punch
makes nice, crisp holes in bond
paper, but the holes only come in
one size. Individual *hole punches*
make "burrless" holes in a variety of papers and other
materials. These finely
tooled circular steel
punches come in a
range of hole sizes and
tool styles, and may be
purchased where
leather-craft supplies are sold. No matter
which tool you use to make the holes in your

Paper trimmer

Hole punching tools

text pages, their diameter should be slightly smaller
than your sewing needle.

To make holes in cover board material, whether
it's paperboard or wood, use either an electric
craft drill or an *eggbeater drill*, which looks like
its namesake. The multipurpose electric craft drill
is versatile and available with many kinds of acces-
sory bits; use either tool to make holes the same size
as the shank of your sewing needle.

Stitching awl

Needles

For the sewing demonstrated in this book, the
basic needle, sometimes called a *tapestry needle*, is
blunt-ended with a large eye. It
will do any of the stitching
you need, but you may
find a curved *uphol-
stery needle* easier
for Coptic binding,
which requires you to
pass the needle behind
some tight stitches.
Both kinds of needles
may be found at any sup-
plier of sewing notions.

Needles

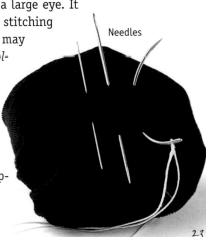

23

Glue brushes

For a tight and secure stitch, the eye of the needle should slightly exceed the diameter of the shank of the awl you use to drill the holes—look for the needle's diameter printed on the package. (For related information on making holes, see Tools for Making Holes, on page 23.)

Note: For Coptic binding, the needle's diameter must not exceed that of the holes in the boards, since the covers are sewn, not glued, to the text block.

Glue Brush

A coarse-bristled, round *glue brush* spreads adhesive quickly and smoothly exactly where you want it. An inexpensive alternative is the disposable foam brush, but resist the temptation to use a paintbrush for gluing—the bristles are too soft for good control. Be sure to have two brushes, one large, one small, to help you glue large sheets and small corners with equal ease. For long brush life, don't dip a dry brush into adhesive. First, get it throughly wet, then blot all the excess moisture on folded paper towels before putting it into the adhesive.

If you use PVA, put the brush in water as soon as you finish applying the glue, or it will quickly fuse the brush's bristles together forever. Before using the brush again, blot out most of the water. To avoid the problem, use wheat paste, which dries more slowly than PVA and can be washed out even after it dries. Use warm water and a mild soap to clean your brushes.

Book Presses, Clamps, and Heavy Weights

Whenever you glue any two materials together, they should dry under weight and pressure. Although the *book press* is the traditional way to do this, inexpensive alternatives are more practical for the amateur journal maker. C-clamps and smooth, hardwood boards make a good substitute, especially when used with a bench vise. If you don't need the tight pressure of clamps, wrap some bricks in soft, clean rag material and use these on top of the pressing boards. Use pieces of scrap board to protect all book materials from pressure marks.

C clamps

Note: The next chapter introduces basic techniques that you'll use to make many of the journals in this book. Only those supplies and tools that are unique to a particular project will be listed at the beginning of each journal's instructions.

Other Tools, Other Books

We've introduced you to the materials and tools you'll need to successfully complete the projects in this book, but there are many books about making books on the market today. These discuss additional supplies and equipment that can be used to make books—some will even tell you how to make your own bookbinding equipment.

The published literature on the craft of making books is hundreds of years old and makes for some fascinating reading.

Book press

TECHNIQUES

In this section you'll find the instructions for basic procedures you'll use to put together your journal. You'll be referred back to this information as needed as you follow the directions for individual projects.

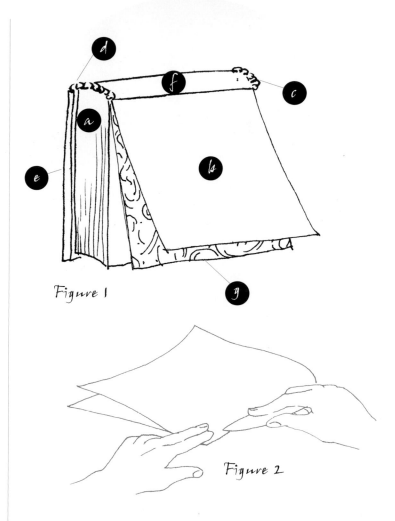

Figure 1

Parts of the Book

These terms identify the basic parts of the book and will help you follow the directions for making any journal project.

The entire gathering of pages known as the *text block* (see figure 1a) is usually faced on both sides with one or more decorative *endpapers* (b). The topmost area of the book is called the *head* (c) and the bottom area is the *tail* (d). Book covers, or *cover boards* (e), protect the text block and support it while it stands on the bookshelf; sometimes these overhang the edges of the block slightly, for better protection of the page edges. The *spine* (f) is that edge of the book where single pages or the edges of the signature folds are joined together, and the opposite side is the *fore edge* (g).

Figure 2

Folding Folios and Making Signatures

In this book, an unfolded sheet of text paper cut to the size that is twice the width of the final page is called a *double text page*. Fold a double text page in half (along the grain, of course) to create a folio. With the corners and edges lined up perfectly, use the bone folder to make a sharp crease, as shown in figure 2. Signatures are created by nesting several folios together.

Making a Decorative Edge

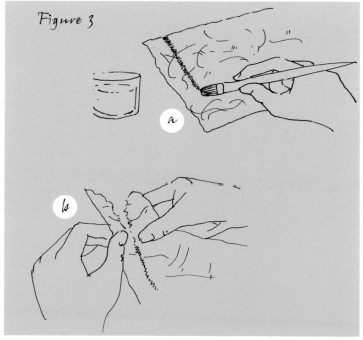

Figure 3

To create a soft, irregular edge on your pages, *wet tear* the paper so it looks like the deckle edge of a fine paper. Using a ruler as a guide, first paint a line of water on the paper (figure 3a). Let it soak in a few moments, then, holding the paper in both hands, tear the paper apart along the line (3b). Be aware that some handmade papers are so strong you can't easily tear them against the grain; instead, wet-tear these papers only along the grain. Vellum cannot be torn at all; cut it instead.

Figure 4

Making Extra Space in the Text Block

If you want to be able to glue bits of printed matter or a pressed flower in your journal, you'll need to add small spacers between some of the text pages. These spacers are referred to by a number of different terms: stubs, spine fatteners, guards, and markers are just a few of them. A spacer can be a very narrow folded strip of sturdy paper sewn into or glued around the signature, as in the Relocation Journal (page 103), or the signatures can rest inside a concertina guard, folded accordion-style, such as in the Gardener's Journal, on page 73. Some of the projects don't have directions for adding spacers, but you can add them to any journal design if you like.

Preparing Signatures for Sewing

It's important that all the holes in the signatures are perfectly aligned with each other. A quick and accurate way to make them is to fashion a template from a narrow scrap of sturdy paper that is the length of the book's spine. Fold it lengthwise, then measure the spacing of the holes and mark their placement with a sharp pencil. To keep the signatures together while you're piercing the holes, lay an opened signature along the bottom edge of a cardboard box, then put the template on top of the signature's fold. Pierce through the template and papers with the awl or pin tool. Or, if you prefer, drill through the opened signature on a flat piece of corrugated cardboard, holding all the pages tightly so they don't slip (see figure 4).

Covering Corners

Boards can be covered with a variety of papers, cloth, or thin leather. Different materials require different corner covering techniques, so the excess material at the edges—called *turn-ins* or *glue tabs*—meets neatly at the corners. Here are step-by-step instructions for covering boards.

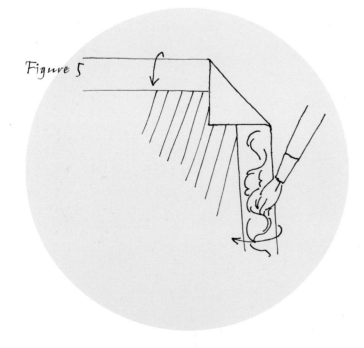

Figure 5

Light- to Medium-Weight Papers and Cloth

1. Brush adhesive over the entire piece of material.

2. Fold the corner triangles down over the board corners, and burnish thoroughly (see figure 5). Apply adhesive to the unglued sections of the exposed cover material, and fold these tabs over, onto the board; burnish thoroughly.

Note: For some tissues and other ultralight materials, you may need to use a heavier liner paper between the tissue and the board, so the board doesn't show through the tissue.

Medium- to Heavyweight Papers and Leather

If the cover material is thick or heavily textured, you'll need to cut away some of the excess material at the corners before turning it in onto the boards.

Method 1

1. Lay the cover board on a piece of cover material that is cut to the correct size. Cut away 45° triangles (as shown in figure 6) from the turn-ins, leaving a square of material at each corner of the board.

2. After gluing, fold the corner piece over the corner of the board, then fold in the turn-ins. Burnish well.

Method 2

1. Stand a scrap of board on edge, so one side of it touches the corner of the cover board as it lays on the cover material. Use a knife to cut a straight line that angles across the corner, as in figure 7a.

2. Brush adhesive on the entire piece of material, then lay the boards in position. Bend the glue tabs around the boards and burnish them thoroughly into place, adding glue to the folded-over corner (see figure 7b). Turn over the cover and burnish the outside.

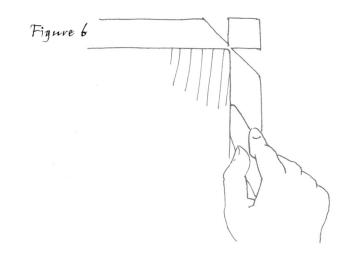

Figure 6

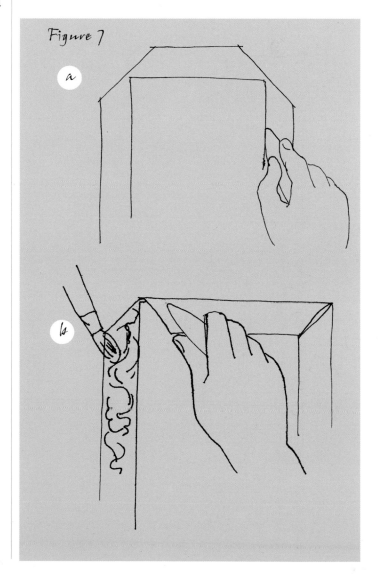

Figure 7

a

b

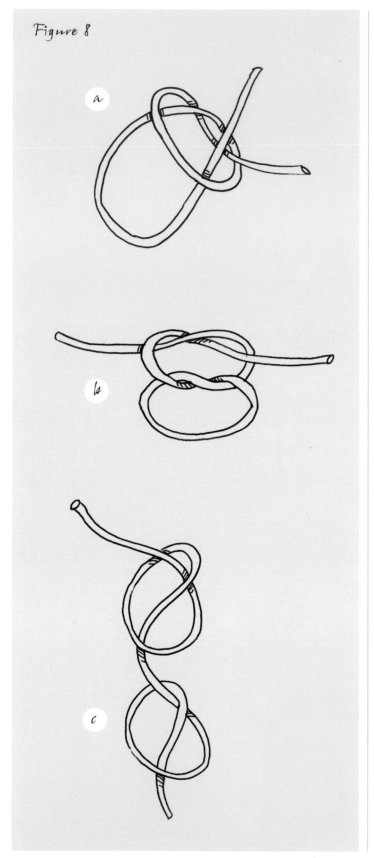

Figure 8

a

b

c

Leather

For best results, use thin, supple leather specially prepared for bookmaking (for more information, read Choosing the Right Cover Material, page 20). Leather turn-ins get bulky in a hurry, so trim them as closely as is practical. If you use a heavier leather, you may want to consult a leather-working book for more information on *skiving*, a leather-thinning process.

Joining Signatures

Once the signatures are folded and pierced with sewing holes, they are stitched together. When the signatures are stacked on top of each other, each single line of sewing holes across the book's spine is called a *station*. When a book's spine is covered by cloth, leather, or paper, such as in the Poet's Journal on page 51, the sewing is an invisible part of the book. The stitching in the Coptic binding method, however, is not only useful but decorative, too. There are several Coptic-bound journals for you to try your hand at—the Gardener's Journal (page 73) and the Quilter's Journal (page 89) are two lively examples of exposed stitching on the spine.

Begin your sewing with a piece of thread the length of your arm. At some point in the middle of your sewing, you'll probably run out of thread. Join the old tail to the new length of thread with a weaver's knot, shown in figure 8a. At the end of the stitching, finish two threads with a square knot (8b) or finish a single thread with a double knot (8c). To keep from tearing the hole open, always pull the needle and thread in the direction of the spine, not perpendicular to it.

You'll be directed back to this section for the sewing instructions in most of the journal projects. Any variations or additional directions are included with each project.

Sewing on Tapes

Linen tape is often sewn across the spine, parallel to the stations, for added strength. It's a good idea to use an odd number of tapes—proportionate to the size of the book—to sew the signatures together. Here are some general guidelines for an average size (approximately 7 x 6 inches or 17.8 x 15.2 cm) book. Book measurements have the height listed first.

1. Use scissors to cut three pieces of bookbinder's tape to the width of the text block *plus* 3 inches (7.6 cm).

2. Cut a piece of scrap paper the height of the text block and 3 inches (7.6 cm) wide. Fold it in half lengthwise. Use this paper to make a pattern to help you pierce perfectly aligned sewing holes in each signature. Find the exact center of the paper by folding it in half. Lay a piece of linen tape across the center point, and make a dot on the crease of the paper, at each side of the tape, as shown in figure 9a.

3. Make a dot on the crease ¹/₂ inch (1.3 cm) down from the top and ¹/₂ inch (1.3 cm) from the bottom of the piece of paper, as in figure 9b. Center the other two pieces of tape between these top and bottom marks and the marks you made on either side of the center tape. Make marks on both sides of these pieces of tape (see figure 9c).

4. Put the template in the fold of the signature. Use the awl to make a hole at each mark.

5. Thread the needle with waxed thread, but don't tie a knot. Pick up one signature and, from the outside, insert the needle into the bottom hole. Come out the second hole; then go back into the signature through the third hole, passing over the first piece of book tape. Continue sewing along the signature, as shown in figure 9d.

6. Pick up the second signature, making sure that the holes line up correctly with those of the first signature. Again, insert the needle from the outside, this time into the first hole at the top. Gently pull the two signatures close to each other by pulling on the thread in the direction of the spine. Come out the second hole, and complete the sewing of this signature just as you did the first one. When you come out of the last hole at the bottom, tie a square knot in the thread (still on the needle) to the tail of thread that extends from the first hole that you entered. Do not cut the thread.

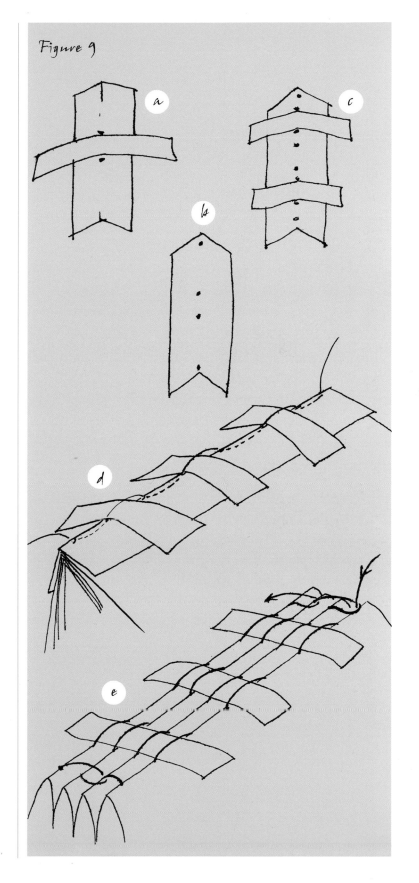

Figure 9

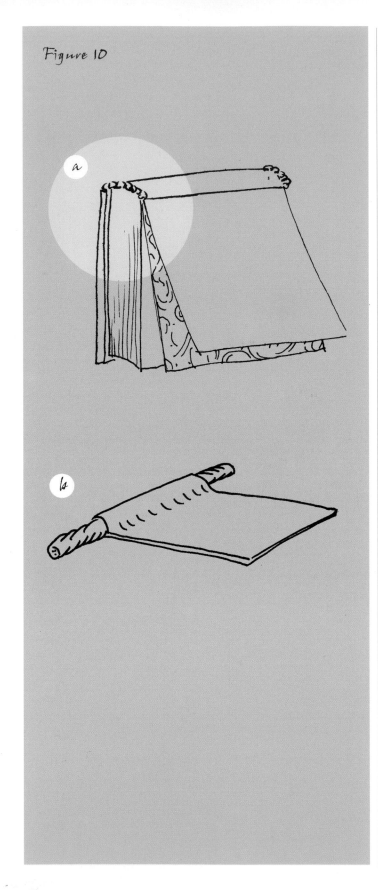

Figure 10

7. Pick up the third signature, and enter into the first hole at the tail, starting from the outside. Continue sewing up to the top, just as you did the other two. When you reach the end of the signature, add the next one, just as you added the others. When you reach the outside of the bottom of this signature, however, pass the needle *behind* the stitch that joins the second and third signatures. Continue sewing in this manner until all the signatures have been added (see figure 9e).

8. When all the signatures are sewn together, tie a double knot on the inside of the last signature.

How to Make a Fake Headband

Headband is a decorative piece of material designed to hide the folds of the signatures at the head and tail of the text block, as shown in figure 10a. Hand-sewn headbands can be quite colorful and are often made with silk thread. Commercially made headband material is available where bookbinding supplies are sold and comes in a variety of colors so you can coordinate it with your cover or endpaper material. If you don't have headband, it's simple to make your own from a small piece of book cloth and a short length of twine.

1. Cut a piece of book cloth 2 x 3 inches (5.1 x 7.6 cm), and cut a piece of twine 3 inches (7.6 cm) long.

2. Fold the cloth lengthwise in half, and place the twine in the crease. Glue the folded cloth together and burnish it so the twine makes a rounded ridge at the crease of the cloth (see figure 10b).

3. Cut the headband with scissors to the width of your finished text block spine.

Note: For Coptic-bound journals, make a Sewn-in Coptic Headband, as described on page 34, instead of gluing on headband.

Assembling the Text Block

This technique describes how to prepare an average-size (7 x 6 inches, or 17.8 x 15.2 cm) text block, adding headbands, endpapers, hinge cloth, and a *spine stiffener* made of sturdy paper. Adjust the measurements as needed if your journal is much larger or smaller than this.

1. Using a glue brush, pound glue into the spine folds of the text block (see figure 11a). Put the text block aside to dry while you cut the hinge, spine stiffener, headbands, and endpapers.

2. To cut the hinge, measure and cut a piece of book cloth ¼ inch (6 mm) less than the height of the book and 3½ inches (8.9 cm) wide. Place the cover boards on each side of the text block, then measure the width of the spine (block and boards) with a ruler. Referring to figure 11b, use the bone folder to make two lengthwise folds in the center of the hinge cloth the same size as the width of the spine. Cut the side flaps of the hinge so they angle in slightly from the folds.

3. Cut a strip of heavy paper the same size as the spine.

4. Using scissors, cut two pieces of headband, each the width of the spine.

5. Cut two endpapers the same size as the double text pages, and fold them into folios. If the papers are decorated on one side, fold them so the decorated side faces inward.

6. Mask off the angled flaps of the book cloth hinge by laying sheets of waste paper right up to the folds. Apply glue to the spine area of the cloth. Discard the waste paper, then lay the gluey hinge onto the block's spine. Burnish it thoroughly, so that it's firmly attached to the spine. The side flaps should be free.

7. Next, glue the piece of spine stiffener paper onto the spine. Glue the headbands at either end of the text block, on top of the spine stiffener, so they extend out a short way from the head and tail of the text block. Figure 11c shows the hinge, headbands, and spine stiffener paper glued to the text block.

8. Use a piece of waste paper with at least one straight edge to mask off all but a ¼-inch-wide (6 mm) strip along the spine edge of the first page of the text block (see figure 11d). Brush glue onto this exposed strip of the page. Discard the waste paper, then press the folded edge of the endpaper folio onto the glue strip, aligning the folio's edges and corners exactly with the edges and corners of the text block. Burnish well over the glued area. Repeat on the other side for the other endpaper.

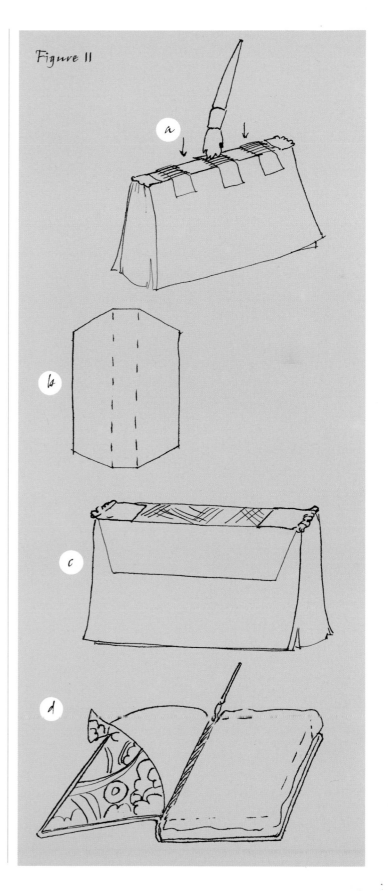

Figure 11

Figure 12

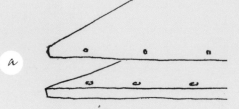

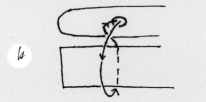

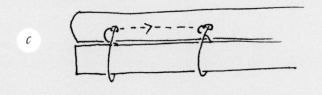

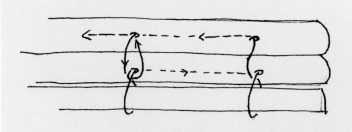

9. Glue the ends of the sewing tapes down to the endpapers next to them. Put wax paper between the glued pages, and set the block aside under heavy weight to dry.

Coptic Binding

Coptic binding is a sewing technique that looks more difficult than it really is. This binding joins the cover boards and signatures with chained stitches all along the stations and makes an attractive decorative element on the exposed spine. You may find it easier to use curved needles, but straight ones will work, too. Here, one- and two-needle methods are shown.

One-Needle Coptic Binding

A simple Coptic binding was used for the Dream Journal on page 43, but various other stitches can be incorporated into this binding method. See the Gardener's Journal on page 73 for inspired stitiching variations.

1. In this example there are six stations; see figure 12a. Thread a needle with a length of waxed thread. To attach the cover to the first signature (as shown in figure 12b), begin sewing (at the head) from the inside of the first signature. Bring the needle around the spine edge of the cover to the outside, entering the hole in the cover from the outside. The needle exits between the inside cover and the first signature, then goes back into the first signature. Now tighten the signature to the cover with a square knot, but do not remove the needle or cut the thread.

2. Take the needle on the inside of the first signature to the next station, then repeat the stitch that joins the cover to the first signature as described in step 1 (see figure 12c).

3. When you sew through the last holes (at the tail) of the cover and the first signature, lay the second signature on top of the first one. Referring to figure 12d, bring the needle out of the inside of the cover and up to the second signature.

4. Continue sewing down the second signature, dropping the needle down to pass under each stitch, as shown in figure 12e. Proceed to step 5 before sewing into the last signature.

5. Lay the last signature above the next to the last signature, then lay the cover on top of it. As you exit the next-to-last signature, bring the needle all the way up to the cover and enter it from the outside, as shown in figure 12f. Exit from inside the cover, then drop the needle down to pass it behind the stitches, as illustrated, before entering the last signature.

6. Continue to sew along the last signature as described in step 5 (see figure 12g).

Two-Needle Coptic Binding

The Relocation Journal on page 103 and the Reunion Journal on page 97 are examples of two-needle Coptic binding. Because the sewing is done with two needles at a time, the sewing holes are referred to as paired stations.

In this example there are three paired stations for a total of six holes; see figure 13a. You have the option of completing the sewing across the entire paired station with a pair of needles before returning to sew the others, or you may complete all the stitching in a signature before adding the next signature. If you sew all the stations in one signature before adding the next one, you'll need as many needles as there are stations in a signature.

1. For each paired station, thread two needles onto a single length of waxed thread. From the inside, insert the needles into the first signature, as shown in figure 13b. Even out the length of thread.

2. To attach the cover to the first signature (as shown in figure 13c, page 34) bring each needle around the spine edge of the cover to the outside, entering the holes in the cover from the outside. The needles exit between the inside cover and the first signature, then go back into the first signature. Tighten the signature to the cover by pulling on the threads in a direction parallel to the spine.

3. Cross the needles on the inside of the first signature, bringing the left needle out the right hole, and the right needle out the left hole, as shown in figure 13d (on page 34).

4. Referring to figure 13e (on page 34), lay the second signature on top of the first one, then bring the pair of needles up from the first signature and into the second one, crossing them on the inside before exiting again.

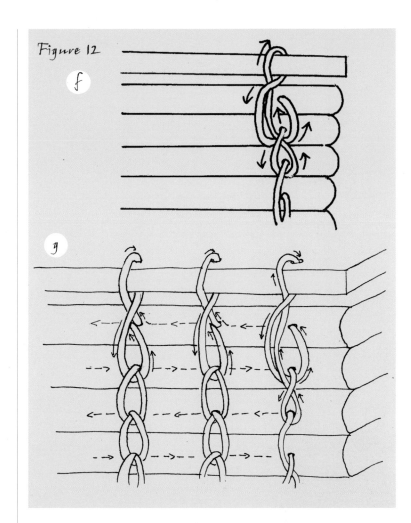

Figure 12
f
g

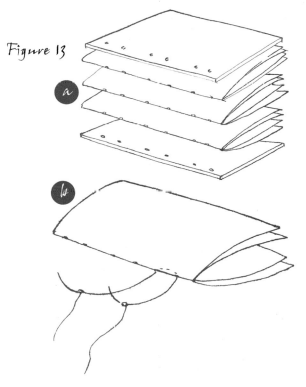

Figure 13
a
b

Figure 13

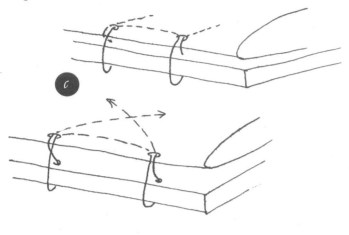

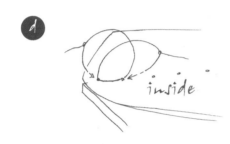

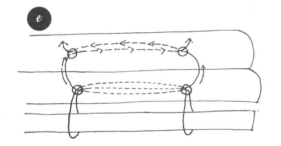

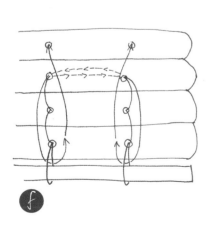

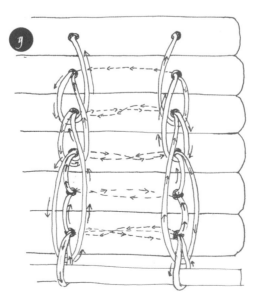

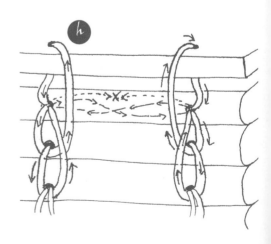

5. After adding the third signature, when the needles are once again on the outside, begin the chained stitch. Drop the left needle down to the space between the cover and the first signature, pass it behind the connecting stitch, then bring the pair of needles up into the stations of the fourth signature (see figure 13f) Continue the stitching pattern, as shown in figure 13g.

6. After adding the last signature and making the chained stitches at the next-to-last signature, do not re-enter the last signature. Instead, attach the back cover, as shown in figure 13h, entering it from the outside. Exit from the inside of the cover, then re-enter the last signature. Tie each pair of threads into a square knot.

Sewn-in Coptic Headbands

Sewing these attractive headbands onto a Coptic-bound journal is optional, but they will make your journal's binding stronger.

1. Thread a tapestry needle with a length of waxed thread. Enter the outermost of the two top holes in the cover, passing the needle from the inside to the outside of the board and leaving a short tail of thread.

2. Re-enter the needle back through the same hole, then pass it under the thread at the edge of the board, as shown in figure 14a.

3. Referring to figure 14b, weave the needle under the threads that cross the top edge of the board, then re-insert the needle from the inside to out.

4. Pass the needle under the latest crossing, from the inside to the out, as shown in figure 14c. Continue the pattern in steps 3 and 4 until about half the space between the two holes in the board is filled, then switch to the next hole (figure 14d).

5. When the stitching fills the distance between the two holes, enter and exit the first station in the first signature, as shown in figure 14e.

6. Pass the needle under the last crossing at the edge of the board, then enter and exit the second signature (see figures 14f and g)

7. Bring the needle under the crossing just created in step 6. Repeat the pattern from steps 6 and 7 across the spine.

8. When you reach the other board, enter from the inside and sew it as you did in steps 1 through 4. Finish the sewing by passing the needle under the stitches on the inside of the board (see figure 14h), then tie a knot in the thread. Neatly glue down the loose tails to the boards. The headband should look like the illustration in figure 14i.

9. Repeat steps 1 through 8 for the other end of the journal.

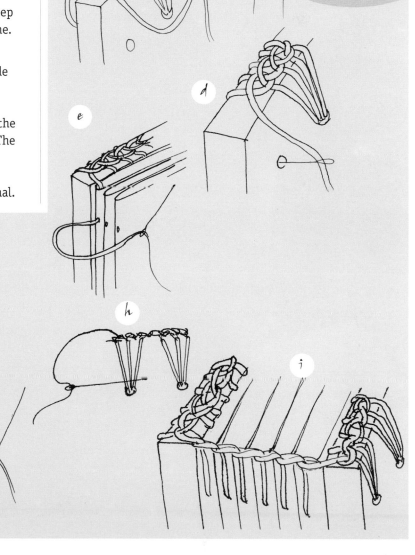

Figure 14

THE PROJECTS

In this part of the book you'll find a wellspring of inspiration for the look and feel of your own journal. Nearly all the techniques, materials, and special details used for any one project may be applied to the journal style that is best suited to your needs.

The designs for most of the books came as the result of a collaboration between a book artist and someone with a hobby or interest such as quilting, poetry, or travel. Each journaler told their partner book artist what they most wanted to see in their journal's design. Once the blank book was finished, it was shipped off to the writer, who began writing. We then borrowed the used journals for a short time, so you'd have a chance to peek over the writer's shoulder and see how they used the finished piece. After your've seen the collaborative journal designs (including a child's journal made at a copy shop), be sure to look at the two blank book projects that follow them. Blank page journals make thoughtful gifts for anyone who likes books.

Once you've made your very own custom book, you'll have a personal, handmade journal that is itself a creative source.

Designer & Journaler:

Gwen Diehn

Designer's and Journaler's Statement: *I made this small, portable travel journal for myself. Its durable cover needed to withstand being packed, pulled out frequently, perhaps rained on, and handled many, many times. I used unlined pages that are good for sketching, and overlays of tracing paper for making notes on top of the drawings. Spine fatteners let me paste in other pieces of paper, leaves, and the like, without causing the fore edge of the book to splay open.*

TRAVEL JOURNAL

This companionable journal has all the elements needed to give the creative journaler a practical, portable volume: a durable cover, unlined pages, and handy tracing-paper overlays. Taking the journal with you wherever you go encourages spontaneous entries, drawings, and collections of memorabilia. Now that designer and journaler Gwen Diehn has returned from her summer trip to Italy, her richly detailed journal entries help her recall the stunning landscapes, fine meals and wines, and remarkable people she met there.

FOR THE TEXT BLOCK

35 sheets of paper, such as drawing paper suitable for pencil, pen, and light watercolor, cut to 5 x 8-inch (12.7 x 20.3 cm) double text pages, and folded into 7 signatures

7 sheets of colored glassine for the tracing pages, cut to 5 x 8-inch (12.7 x 20.3 cm) double text pages, interleaved with text pages and spine fatteners as described below. If you can't find the glassine, use tracing paper or parchment instead.

7 pieces of heavy paper (scraps of charcoal paper work well), cut to 5 x 3 inches (12.7 x 7.6 cm) each, folded lengthwise for spine fatteners

1 small piece of heavy paper, cut to the size of the spine of the text block, for spine stiffener

2 sheets of decorative paper, cut to 5 x 8-inch (12.7 x 20.3 cm) double text pages, for endpapers

3 pieces of bookbinder's tape, 3 inches (7.6 cm) wide

Book cloth, 6 x 6 inches (15.2 x 15.2 cm)

Headband

FOR THE COVER

1 piece thin, supple leather, cut to 5³⁄₄ x 10¹⁄₄ inches (14.7 x 26.1 cm); this allows for a ³⁄₄-inch (1.9 cm) spine and a ¹⁄₄-inch (6 mm) overhang of the text block

2 pieces of archival cardboard, cut to 5¹⁄₄ x 4¹⁄₄ inches (13.4 x 10.9 cm)

Archival cardboard, cut to 5¹⁄₄ x ³⁄₄ inches (13.4 x 1.9 cm), for the spine

SUPPLIES

Linen tape

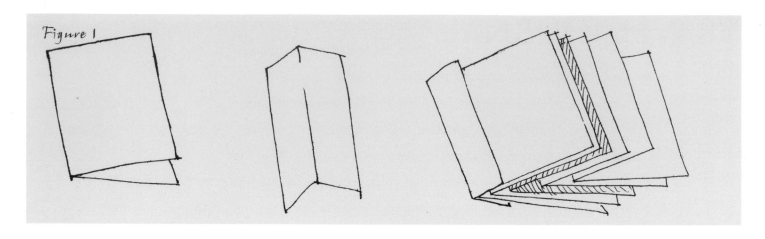

Figure 1

Figure 2

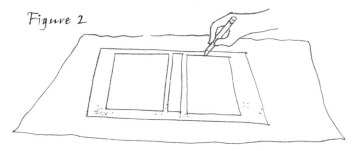

1 Fold each spine fattener in half lengthwise, using the bone folder to make a crisp fold.

2 Interleave the papers for the text block. Each signature begins with a spine fattener, then two folios of text paper, a folio of glassine, and another two folios of text paper, as shown in figure 1.

3 Sew the signatures together using the tape sewing technique described on page 29.

4 Assemble the text block with the book hinge, endpapers, and headbands, as described on page 30.

Figure 3

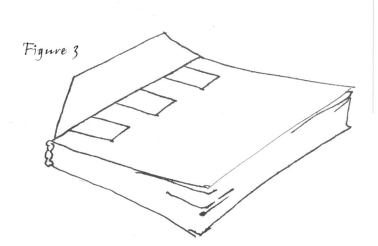

Figure 4

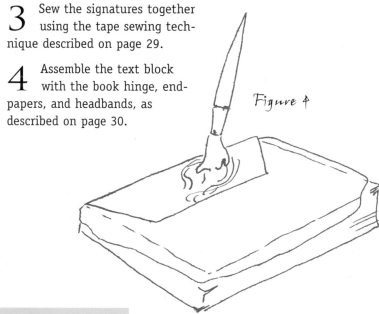

Making the Cover

1 Lay the piece of leather (with the inside of the leather facing up) on a piece of scrap paper. Assemble the two cover boards and the spine board, as shown in figure 2. Mark the leather to show where the pieces must be placed. Allow a ¼ inch (6 mm) gap between each piece of board.

2 Remove the boards and brush glue over the entire piece of leather. Carefully place the boards on the glue-covered material. Maintain the ¼ inch (6 mm) gap for the entire length of the spaces between the boards and the spine, or the book will be too tight to open and close easily. Burnish all the glued-together surfaces.

3 Use one of the methods for Covering Corners described on page 27 for heavy and textured cover material.

Joining the Cover to the Text Block

1 Glue the ends of the tapes to the endpapers (see figure 3). Then brush glue onto the outside of one hinge flap, as in figure 4.

2 Carefully center the spine on the spine board. Hold the text block so it stands straight up while you burnish the hinge flap to the boards; see figure 5. Be sure to press the cloth into the crevice between the spine and cover board, as shown in figure 6. Repeat for the other hinge flap.

3 Brush glue all over the outside of the endpaper (see figure 7). Hold the spine of the text block flat against the spine board while you fold the gluey endpaper down and burnish it to the inside of the cover board. Repeat this step for the other endpaper.

4 Put pieces of wax paper between the inside covers and text block, and press the book under a pile of heavy books for a couple of hours. Be sure to let the spine hang out beyond the edges of the heavy books; see figure 8.

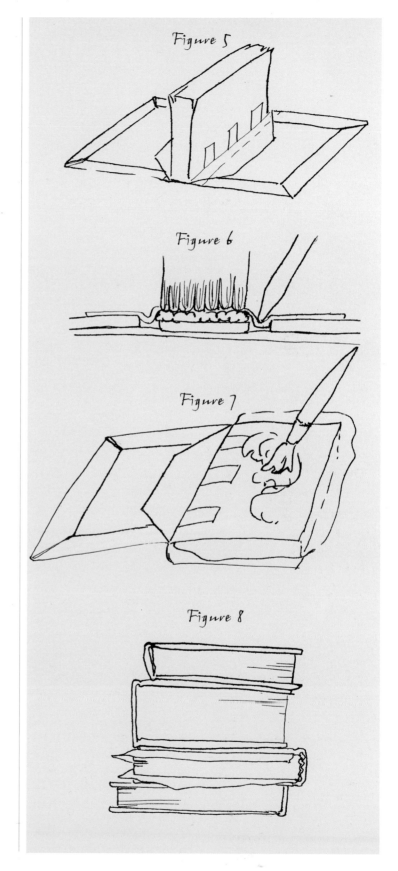

Figure 5

Figure 6

Figure 7

Figure 8

Designer:
Benares Finan-Eshelman

Journaler:
Candace Stoumen

Designer's Statement: *I found it challenging to create a personal journal for someone I had only interacted with a few times, but we had similar approaches to our journaling styles and that helped me to integrate my asthetic with her needs. Candace likes to have access to a variety of materials when she sits down to journal. I settled on creating a bag that could hold the journal and all the tools and materials she might want to keep with it. I chose a versatile drawing and writing paper for the journal because I have found that an important facet of journaling is having the space and freedom within the structure of a book to use its pages in the most effective manner possible. The colors (reds, blues, and blacks) are some that I consider powerful and relevant to dreams, and I hoped they might provide inspiration for Candace's entries.*

Journaler's Statement: *This journal designed especially for me is a sacred object. It is exactly what I want to use for my poems, dreams, and art images. I love the size, the texture of the paper, and the construction of the book. The red journal is my friend and I am inspired to express myself on each page.*

DREAM JOURNAL

Despite its dreamy, ephemeral subject matter, this journal has a strong presence, with its generous, squared pages and bold, symbolic colors. The Coptic binding makes the pages lie flat, for easy writing. Each signature is enclosed by a piece of heavy black paper to remind the journaler of the night flights into her own subconscious. Designer Benares Finan-Eshelman sewed a loose pouch from black cotton to protect the beautiful tissue-paper covers and to give journaler Candace Stoumen a place to store writing utensils, glitter glue, and the like. Not incidentally, it keeps her writings under wraps!

FOR THE TEXT BLOCK

32 sheets of speckled oatmeal-colored paper, cut to 9 x 18-inch (22.9 x 45.7 cm) double text pages, folded into 8 signatures

8 sheets of medium-weight black paper, cut to 9 x 18-inch (22.9 x 45.7 cm) double text pages, folded into the outermost folio for each signature

FOR THE COVER

4 sheets of handmade red tissue paper, cut to 10$\frac{1}{2}$ x 10$\frac{1}{2}$ inches (26.7 x 26.7 cm), for the covers

2 pieces book board, cut to 9$\frac{1}{2}$ x 9$\frac{1}{2}$ inches (24.1 x 24.1 cm), for the covers

SUPPLIES AND TOOLS

Scrap piece of bond paper, cut to 9 x 3 inches (22.9 x 7.6 cm), for the sewing template

Black waxed thread

I've dreamed in my life dreams that have stayed with me even after, and changed my ideas: they've gone through and through me, like wine through water, and altered the color of my mind.

Emily Brontë

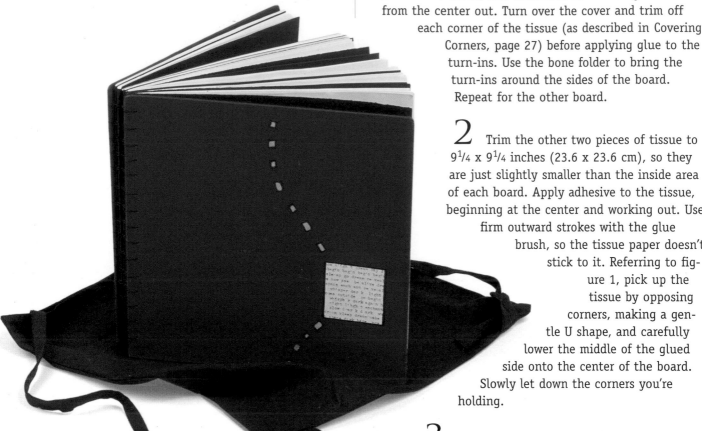

1 Lay out the cover board, and apply the PVA to it, brushing it out from the center. Carefully lay the red tissue on the board, and smooth it down with your hands from the center out. Turn over the cover and trim off each corner of the tissue (as described in Covering Corners, page 27) before applying glue to the turn-ins. Use the bone folder to bring the turn-ins around the sides of the board. Repeat for the other board.

2 Trim the other two pieces of tissue to 9¼ x 9¼ inches (23.6 x 23.6 cm), so they are just slightly smaller than the inside area of each board. Apply adhesive to the tissue, beginning at the center and working out. Use firm outward strokes with the glue brush, so the tissue paper doesn't stick to it. Referring to figure 1, pick up the tissue by opposing corners, making a gentle U shape, and carefully lower the middle of the glued side onto the center of the board. Slowly let down the corners you're holding.

3 Wrap the boards in wax paper and press them under a heavy weight until they are thoroughly dry.

4 Make a paper template from a piece of scrap paper that is 9 inches (22.9 cm) long, the same size as the height of the spine. Fold it in half lengthwise, then fold it in half in the other direction, and continue to fold the ends in to the center until you have 15 folds (see figure 2).

5 Unfold the paper and make a mark at each of the crosswise fold lines. Put this template inside the fold of each signature, and pierce all the way through the five folios. Repeat this step for all the signatures.

6 Stack the two cover boards on top of each other with their front sides facing up. Again, fold the template in half lengthwise, and lay it alongside the spine side of the board, ¼ inch (6 mm) from the edge. Use the template as a guide to pierce the sewing holes into the boards. Using firm pressure, push the awl through the top board just hard enough to make a mark with the pointed end of

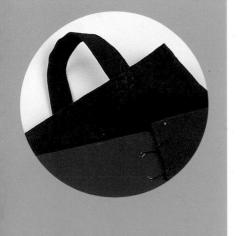

Figure 1

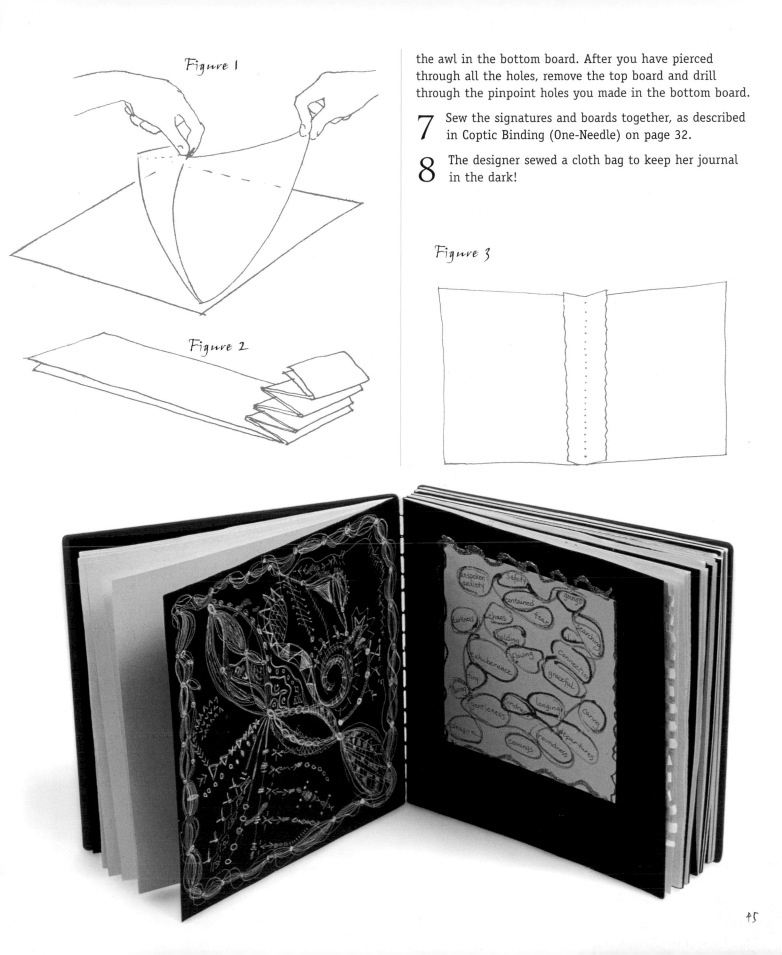

Figure 2

Figure 3

the awl in the bottom board. After you have pierced through all the holes, remove the top board and drill through the pinpoint holes you made in the bottom board.

7 Sew the signatures and boards together, as described in Coptic Binding (One-Needle) on page 32.

8 The designer sewed a cloth bag to keep her journal in the dark!

Designer:
Gwen Diehn

Journaler:
Catharine Sutherland

Designer's Statement: *Catharine wanted a book that had fairly large pages—some made of tracing paper, so she could trace yoga asanas into her journal. She wanted a soft, light cover that felt cool and breezy in her hands. She was getting ready to move to the southwest United States, and she wanted the colors to remind her of the desert and the southwestern sky.*

Journaler's Statement: *The page sizes are great; plenty of room for detailed drawings and I can be very expressive, saying as much or as little as I want to say. The journal style gives me a lot of freedom; I don't have to keep certain dates on certain pages—I can flip around however I want. The vellum paper in back is perfect for tracing positions from the many different yoga books I have; allowing me to carry just one book of my favorite poses. The journal is easy to write in because it lays flat; it's not rigid, but nice and loose-feeling. The beachy colors and calm subtle tones suggest freedom and openess, like where I'm going to move.*

YOGA JOURNAL

Since yoga is a discipline that requires a lot of physical flexibility, journaler Catharine Sutherland wanted a journal that fit into that philosophy: easy and casual, yet imaginatively responsive. The soft cover lets her roll it up in a backpack (she rolls up her exercise mat), the large pages invite a loose calligraphic style of expression, and the overlay sheets are big enough for her to slip the instructions for an entire movement sequence under them, so she can copy them from previous journals.

FOR THE TEXT BLOCK

28 sheets of medium-weight drawing paper, cut to 12$\frac{1}{2}$ x 19-inch (31.8 x 48.3 cm) double text pages, and folded into 7 signatures

7 sheets of vellum or tracing paper, cut to 12$\frac{1}{2}$ x 19-inch (31.8 x 48.3 cm) double text pages, and folded into 7 signatures, interleaved with the drawing paper folios (Note: Vellum pages must be cut, not torn.)

FOR THE COVER

Cloth placemat (a woven cotton mat measuring 13$\frac{1}{2}$ x 19$\frac{1}{2}$ inches [34.3 x 49.5 cm] was used in this example)

SUPPLIES AND TOOLS

Heavy upholstery needle, or use a heavy-duty sewing machine

4 metal clips, such as bulldog clips

Beads

With an eye made quiet by the power of harmony, and the deep power of joy, we see into the life of things.
William Wordsworth

Figure 1

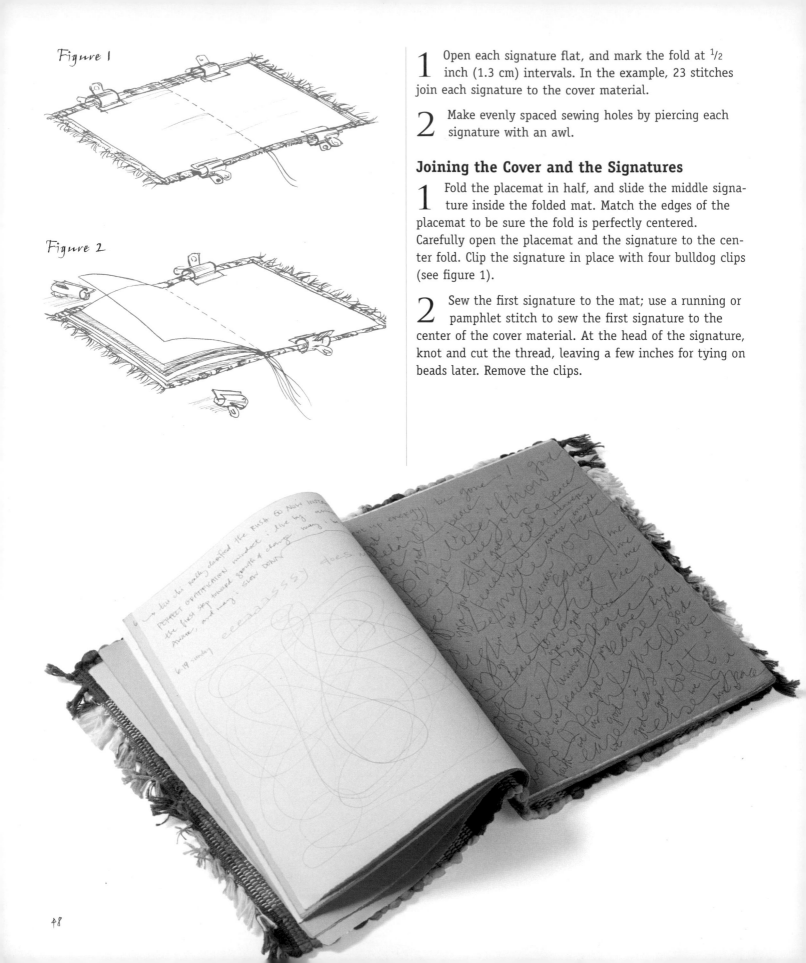

1 Open each signature flat, and mark the fold at $^1/_2$ inch (1.3 cm) intervals. In the example, 23 stitches join each signature to the cover material.

2 Make evenly spaced sewing holes by piercing each signature with an awl.

Joining the Cover and the Signatures

1 Fold the placemat in half, and slide the middle signature inside the folded mat. Match the edges of the placemat to be sure the fold is perfectly centered. Carefully open the placemat and the signature to the center fold. Clip the signature in place with four bulldog clips (see figure 1).

2 Sew the first signature to the mat; use a running or pamphlet stitch to sew the first signature to the center of the cover material. At the head of the signature, knot and cut the thread, leaving a few inches for tying on beads later. Remove the clips.

3 Slide the next signature in, to one side of the center signature. Open this signature to its center, and clip it to the cover material as you did for the first signature (see figure 2).

4 Sew the center seam of the second signature the same way you did the first one, again leaving extra thread at the top end of the seam.

5 Repeat step 3 for all the signatures, placing them on alternating sides of the sewn signatures, until all of them are sewn into the book, as shown in figure 3.

6 Unravel the ends of the extra thread. Divide the lengths of thread into three bunches. Twist each bunch tightly enough that the thread ends will go through a bead (see figure 4).

7 Push the bead tightly against the cloth cover, then divide the threads in two groups as they leave the bead; tie them into a double knot, as in figure 5. Trim the threads to a 1 inch (2.5 cm) length. Repeat for each of the other two beads.

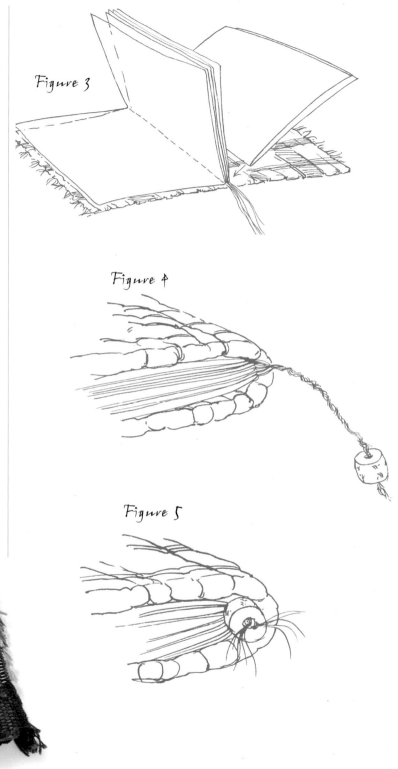

Figure 3

Figure 4

Figure 5

Designer:
Gwen Diehn

Journaler:
Ann Turkle

Designer's Statement: Ann wanted three books in one. The size of the main journal is similar to that of the ruled notebooks she has always used as journals. She also wanted a small portable journal that could fit into the main journal when she was at hom,e but could just as easily slip it into her pocket, to accompany her on her daily rounds. Finally, she wanted a place to save words, possibly as an alphabetized section of the main book.

Journaler's Statement: *Beware of getting what you ask for. Gwen gave me, so perfectly, what I said a "poet's journal" should be, though it was a little intimidating to begin using it. Gwen and I were traveling with students, and that trip helped me leap into the journal, to mimic my students. (I wonder how often that is true and how often teachers are reluctant to admit it.) Since my poetry is both visual and narrative, recording and actually pasting visual memorabilia into the journal was a useful activity to me.*

POET'S JOURNAL

Designer Gwen Diehn's clever construction holds three books in one, using a dos à dos ("back to back") structure. As a poet, journaler Ann Turkle likes to collect and use words, so this journal works the way she does. The largest volume has the right feel for writing at a desk, and its companion "poet's dictionary", on the other side of the shared cover board, helps word lovers make notations for future reference. The smallest book is pocket-sized for spontaneous observations when you're on the go.

FOR THE THREE TEXT BLOCKS

35 pieces of text-weight paper, cut to $9^{1}/_{4}$ x $14^{1}/_{4}$-inch (23.5 x 36.2 cm) double text pages for the largest book; folded into 7 signatures

25 sheets of laid text paper in a variety of soft colors, cut to 5 x $14^{1}/_{2}$-inch (12.7 x 36.8 cm) double text pages; folded into 5 signatures, for the half-size book with tabbed pages

25 sheets of laid text paper, cut to 6 x 8-inch (15.2 x 20.3 cm) double text pages; folded into 5 signatures, for the small book that slips into the space above the half-size book

6 pieces of decorative fabric for endpapers for each of the books, cut to the same size as their respective double text pages

Decorative fabric, cut to $9^{1}/_{4}$ x $14^{1}/_{4}$-inch (23.5 x 36.2 cm) double text page, for the endpaper of the largest text block

9 pieces of bookbinder's tape, each 3 inches (7.6 cm) long

Headband

FOR THE COVERS

2 pieces of archival cardboard, cut to $9^{1}/_{2}$ inches (24.1 cm) long, and as wide as the spines of the largest and medium-size sewn text blocks (don't cut the spine boards until you've sewn the blocks)

3 pieces of archival cardboard, cut to $9^{1}/_{2}$ x $7^{1}/_{2}$ inches (24.1 x 19.1 cm), for the largest covers

Thin, supple leather, cut to 12 x 4 inches (30.5 x 10.2 cm), for the spine (or substitute book cloth of a contrasting color); and 6 x 13 inches (15.2 x 33 cm), for the cover of the smallest book

Strip of decorative paper, cut to 12 x 2 inches (30.5 x 5.1 cm)

2 pieces of book cloth, cut to 12 x $8^{1}/_{2}$ inches (30.5 x 21.6 cm); and 12 x $19^{1}/_{2}$ (30.5 x 49.5 cm), for the largest covers

Decorative fabric, cut to $11^{1}/_{2}$ x 1 inches (29.2 x 2.5 cm), to cover the largest spine

2 pieces of decorative fabric, cut to $9^{1}/_{4}$ x $7^{1}/_{4}$ inches (23.5 x 18.4 cm), for the insides of two of the largest covers

Stand still, true poet that you are!
Robert Browning

Note: Sew the three text blocks, following the directions in the section Sewing on Tapes, page 29. The second and third books must be of the same thickness, so the journal will close evenly.

Making the Covers

1 Cut two spine boards for the largest covers. To measure the needed width, slightly compress the sewn text block between two cover boards, and measure from outside edge to outside edge.

2 The piece of spine-covering leather should be about 3 inches (7.6 cm) more than the width of the spine. Brush the leather with glue. Carefully lay the wider of the two spine boards down the center of the piece of leather, then lay a 9½-inch (24.1 cm) cover board along each side of the spine board. Leave a ¼ inch (6 mm) gap between all pieces, as shown in figure 1.

3 Wrap the excess leather around the front of the boards and burnish it thoroughly, so the leather sticks completely to the boards. Use a bone folder to press the leather against the edges of the boards as well as the flat surfaces. Turn over the boards and burnish the other side.

4 To cover the front of the largest text block, turn the cover so the leather-covered spine is facing up. Glue the strip of decorative paper to the left-hand side of the cover board. Be sure to butt the long edge of the strip up against the leather, then wrap the extra paper around top and bottom as you did with the leather strip (figure 2). Burnish both sides thoroughly.

5 Brush glue all over the inside of the 12 x 8½-inch (30.5 x 20.3 cm) piece of book cloth, and carefully line up and place a perfectly straight edge of the book cloth ⅛ inch (3 mm) out from the strip of leather, so the decorative paper shows between them. There should be about an inch of overlap at the top and bottom of the board, as shown in figure 3. Burnish, then turn the cover over.

6 Fold a triangle of book cloth over each of the two corners. Add more glue as needed, and fold the glue tabs onto the cover, completely wrapping the edges (figure 4). Burnish thoroughly.

7 Turn the already-covered section of the book so its insides face up. Brush glue all over the other piece of book cloth. Carefully lay this gluey book cloth over the pieces of board, lining up the left-hand edge of the cloth

Figure 1

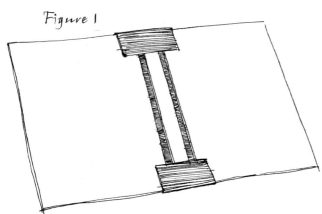

Figure 2

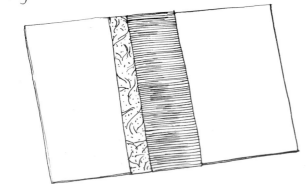

with the right-hand edge of the leather spine cover, and keep the boards separated by $1/4$ inch (6mm) gaps (see figure 5). Burnish, being very careful to keep the boards in place under the book cloth.

8 Carefully turn over the boards. Realign the spine and cover board if they shifted out of position. Above all, be sure the bottoms are lined up perfectly straight and the $1/4$ inch (6 mm) gaps remain. Then, fold in the corners and the glue tabs, as shown in figure 6. Burnish everything.

9 Fold the cover into a Z, as in figure 7.

Joining the Cover to the Largest Text Block

1 To glue the large text block to the leather-covered spine section of the book, first brush glue onto the outside of the front spine hinge flap, as shown in figure 8 on page 54.

2 Stand the spine (which is not glued) onto the exact center of the spine board, and press the gluey hinge flap into place. Burnish the hinge flap into any gaps, as well as onto the cover; see figure 9 on page 54. Repeat for the other hinge flap.

3 Brush glue over the outside of the endpaper fabric for the front of the large text block. Carefully close the cover to position the paper onto the board. Open the cover to burnish, being sure to burnish into the fold. Repeat for the back endpaper fabric (see figure 10 on page 54).

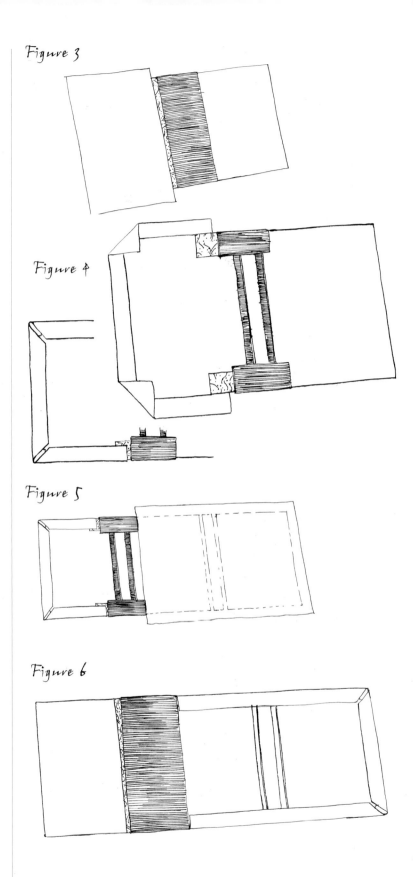

Figure 3

Figure 4

Figure 5

Figure 6

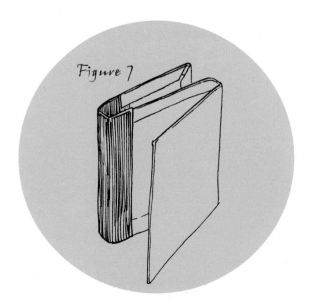

Figure 7

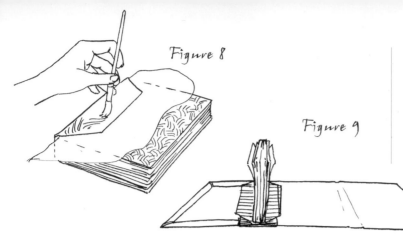

Figure 8

Figure 9

Figure 10

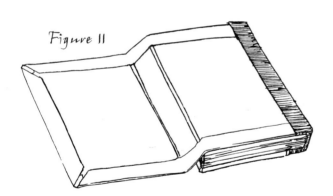

Figure 11

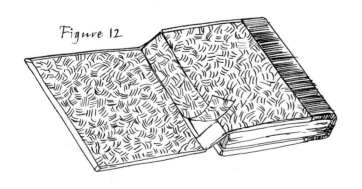

Figure 12

4 To glue the medium-size text block in, close the large text block cover and turn the journal over, so the inside of the other cover is open to your left, as shown in figure 11.

5 Glue the two page-sized piece of fabric to the insides of the two remaining cover boards. The spine board is still exposed.

6 Cut the strip of endpaper fabric over the exposed spine board, between the already glued pieces of endpaper (figure 12). Burnish everything.

Joining the Cover to the Medium-Size Text Block

1 Glue in the medium-size text block the same way you did for the largest block. Be sure to line up the medium-size text block with the bottom of the journal (figure 13).

2 Each tab will be ½ inch (1.3 cm) wide and one-ninth the height of the text block. To cut the alphabet tabs, divide the height of the medium-size text block pages by 9. Referring to figure 14, lightly draw a pencil line on the first page where the bottom of the first tab will be. Draw another line ½ inch (1.3 cm) in from the edge.

3 Divide the number of pages in the text block by 9; this is how many pages there will be in each tabbed section. Slip a piece of light cardboard underneath the bottom sheet of the first tabbed section. Use a ruler and mat knife to cut through all the sheets in the

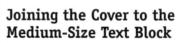

Figure 13

section at one time. It is better to make several light passes with the knife rather than try to cut through them all at once.

4 Remove the cardboard. Continue to use this method to draw and cut the rest of the tabs. When all tabs are cut, letter the first page of each tabbed section with three letters of the alphabet.

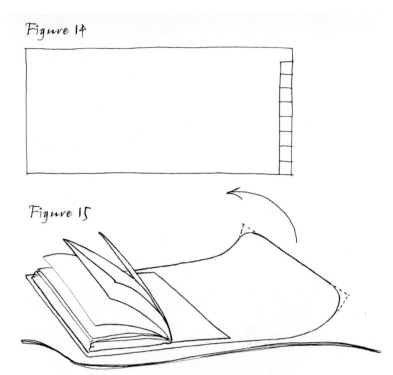

Figure 14

Figure 15

Joining the Cover to the Smallest Text Block

1 Lay out the leather for the cover, and set the spine of the smallest book on it; mark the placement of the spine on the leather. Position the block to allow a ½ inch (1.3 cm) of leather to hang over the fore edge of the block.

Using a protective sheet of wax paper under it, apply glue to the first text page. Burnish this page directly to the leather cover.

2 Cut curved edges on the top flap, as shown in figure 15.

3 Fold the book, securing it with a thin strip of leather. Slip the removable book into the space above the tabbed-paged text block.

Designer:
Coral Jensen

Journaler:
Bobbe Needham

Designer's Statement: *Bobbe wanted a colorful journal and album with easy access to the pages (ability to take out and add pages). I wanted to create a design that was reminiscent of childhood and sturdy enough to withstand a lot of handling. I decided that wood covers and a screw post binding suited all the journaler's criteria. To add to the fun of the book, I decided to use a variety of papers for its pages; some of them are heavy enough to mount photographs or to do a collage treatment.*

GRANDMOTHER'S JOURNAL

This playful-looking journal helps anyone who loves a child write and reminisce in this fun yet practical design. Designer Coral Jensen chose a screw post binding that let journaler Bobbe Needham add or remove pages and paste in photos with ease. Richly colored plain and origami interior pages invite whimsical entries from a light and loving heart.

FOR THE TEXT BLOCK

24 sheets card stock and text-weight papers, cut to $4^5/8$ x 6 inches (11.8 x 15.2 cm)

FOR THE COVER

2 pieces of hardwood board, each cut to $3/8$ x $4^3/4$ x 6 inches (9.5 mm x 10.2 x 15.2 cm). (In the example, hickory was used for all the wood pieces, but a softer wood, like poplar, works as well.)

5 pieces of decorative paper: 2 strips, cut to $1/4$ x 2 inches (6 mm x 5.1 cm) each; 2 strips, cut to $1/4$ x $3^1/2$ inches (6 mm x 8.9 cm) each; and 1 rectangular piece, cut to $5^3/4$ x $4^1/2$ inches (14.7 x 11.4 cm)

2 strips of wood, cut to $3/8$ x 6 x 1 inches (9.5 mm x 15.2 x 2.5 cm)

Small round dollhouse mirror, $7/8$ inch (2.2 cm) in diameter

30 dollhouse nails $2^1/4$ x $3^1/4$-inch (5.8 x 8.3

cm) heavyweight acetate or transparency material (available at a photocopy shop or office-supply store), for the inside of the front cover

1 small package of white, clear, or natural color polymer clay

Small piece of thin leather, about 1 inch long, for the hinge

2 dollhouse hinges

Wooden skewer, $1/16$ inch (1.6 mm) in diameter

Liquid acrylic paints, in a variety of colors

Leather cording, 24 inches (61 cm) long

Assortment of decorative beads in different colors

3 brass or aluminum screw posts, $1/4$ x $1^5/8$ inches (6 mm x 4.1 cm)

SUPPLIES AND TOOLS

Gouge (a wood-carving tool) with a narrow sweep or curve

Electric handheld multipurpose or power drill, with $1/8$-inch (3 mm) and $1/4$-inch (6 mm) bits

Coping or jeweler's saw

Small carving tool, such as a skew chisel, or a handheld electric multipurpose tool with a barrel-shaped carving tool attachment

Sandpaper, 125- and 220-grit

Small hammer, for the dollhouse nails

Dull butter knife or other clay-cutting tool

Cyanoacrylate gel adhesive

Yellow carpenter's glue

Small paintbrush

Plastic paint palette

Paper punch (available at office supply stores)

Making the Covers

1 Use the gouge to create texture in the two wooden cover pieces.

2 For the small window in the front cover, measure and mark a 2^7/$_8$ x 2-inch (7.3 x 5.1 cm) rectangle on it. Use the ^{1}/$_8$-inch (3 mm) bit to drill a hole in the center of the rectangle. Insert the blade of the coping saw into the hole, and cut out a rough opening (see figure 1). Scallop the edges of the opening if you wish. Finish the opening by carving a narrow lip inside its perimeter with the chisel, as shown in figure 2.

3 Trace around the dollhouse mirror to mark a circle in the back cover. Use the chisel to carve out the circle to a depth of ^{1}/$_8$ to ^{1}/$_4$ inch (3 to 6 mm). With the gouge, carve a surface design around the mirror (figure 3).

4 Sand smooth all the edges of the wood pieces; start with the 125-grit sandpaper, then finish with the 220-grit paper. Use the gel adhesive to glue the mirror into the carved out circle.

5 Using the dollhouse nails, tack the sheet of heavy-weight acetate over the opening in the inside of the front cover (see figure 4).

Figure 1

Figure 2

Figure 3

Figure 4

6 To fashion a door, roll the polymer clay into a slab 2⅞ x 2 x ⅛ inches (7.3 x 5.1 cm x 3 mm). Use the dull butter knife to trim the clay to the same size as the lip of the cover's opening, as shown in figure 5. Follow the instructions on the package for working and baking the clay. When the clay door has hardened and cooled, sand the edges smooth, making sure it fits neatly into the cover.

7 For the closure on the door, first punch a small hole into one end of the strip of leather (figure 6). If you don't have a suitable punch, ask a shoe repair shop to do it. Then drill a 1/8-inch (3 mm) hole into the door to hold the leather strip. Knot the other end of the strip of leather, then thread it through the hole, as shown in figure 7.

8 To attach the door to the front cover, first adhere the doll hinges with the gel adhesive, then put it under a heavy weight until dry. When the adhesive has dried, hammer the small nails into the holes of the hinges.

9 Drill a small pilot hole, about 1/16 inch (1.6 mm) deep, into the front cover, aligning this hole with the one you made in the door for the handle. Cut a ⅛-inch (3 mm) piece of the skewer and use the yellow glue to set it into the hole you just drilled into the cover (see figure 8).

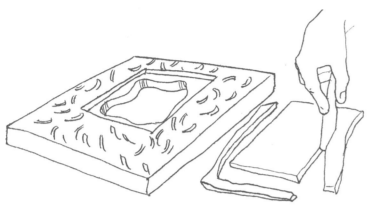

Figure 5

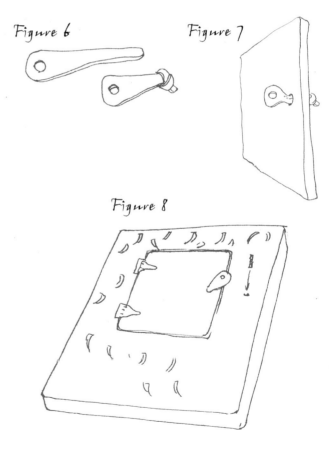

Figure 6

Figure 7

Figure 8

Putting the Parts of the Covers Together

1 The length and diameter of the screw posts you use is optional, as long as the size of your drill bit matches that of the posts, for a snug fit. In the example, the designer used a ¼-inch (6 mm) diameter bit and posts. Drill three evenly spaced holes into the 6 x ¾ x ⅜-inch (2.5 x 15.2 cm x 9.5 mm) strips of wood, as shown in figure 9, for the posts.

2 Mix the acrylics with water, and apply light washes to all the wood pieces and to the door, creating soft layers of color.

3 Referring to figures 10a and b, carefully measure and mark six holes on the sides of the two wood strips. Using a ⅛-inch (3 mm) bit, drill all the way through the width of the strips. On each of the covers, mark six holes that correspond to the ones you made in the two strips, ⅛ inch (3 mm) from the left edge.

4 To join the two cover pieces, knot the length of leather cord, then thread several decorative beads onto it. Knot the cord again and, from the outside, thread it through the hole at the tail, sewing the pieces together, as shown in figures 11a and b. When you finish sewing the head, knot in some beads as you did at the tail. Repeat the lacing process for the other two cover pieces.

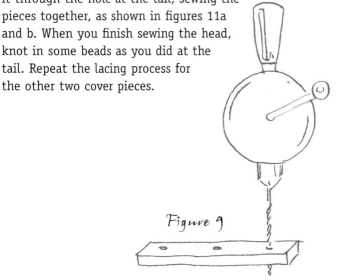

Figure 9

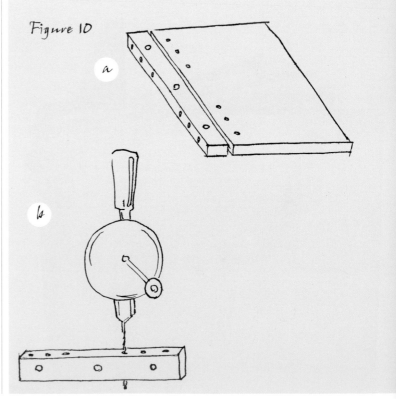

Figure 10

a

b

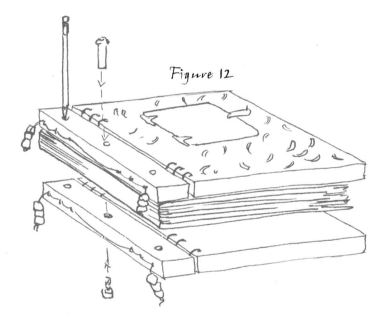

Joining the Covers to the Text Block

1 Neatly stack the text pages. Line up one of the wood strips at the left edge of the top sheet of paper. Mark through the post holes with a pencil, then use the awl to drill holes in all the text pages. See figure 12.

2 Assemble the covers and text pages; put the posts through them, then attach the screw ends to the post ends.

3 Use the craft glue to adhere the strips of decorative paper over the edges of the acetate window. Glue the rectangular piece of decorative paper to the inside of the back cover, as an endpaper.

Figure 12

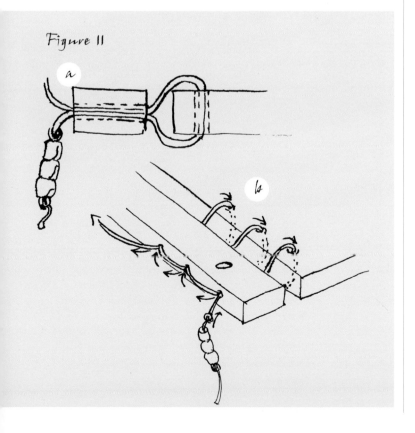

Figure 11

a

b

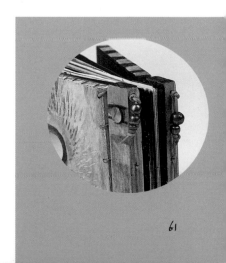

> *"Nature without exercise is a seed shut up in a pod, and art without practice is nothing."*
>
> Pietro Aretino

Designer:
Dan Essig

Journaler:
Wonder Koch

Designer's Statement: *I was familiar with Wonder's work and wanted to create a journal that would fit her style of layered designs and three-dimensional art. I chose white paper to give a feeling of openness to the journaler's creative vision. The seemingly endless structure of this book is made from a combination of accordian folds (nothing is glued or fastened), because I wanted Wonder to be able to manipulate the book to fit her needs and to give her a variety of display options.*

Journaler's Statement: *As in any collaborative work, there was an energy that comes from working with someone else. The function of collaboration for me has always been to create something beyond what one could make alone. I enjoyed the mysterious result that neither party could foresee. At first, I was afraid to write in the book because it was made specifically for me and the pages were so white and clean, so I just wrote anything on them, and started layering over them with words and gesso.*

SCULPTURE JOURNAL

This three-dimensional journal is constructed from folded paper only—no sewing! Create a journal whose form can change shape at a whim. This versatile design can be viewed as a traditional book, or displayed as a sculptural object in its own right. Use a rich, soft, and flexible paper that can take plenty of ink and paste if you want to try a multimedia approach to journaling. You can allow for small variations in measurements by cutting the boards after you cut and fold the text paper to its final size.

FOR THE TEXT BLOCK

3 pieces of medium-weight paper, 17 x 28³/₄ inches (43.2 x 73.1 cm), cut as described below, for the text pages

FOR THE COVER

2 pieces of charcoal or other sturdy paper, cut to 13¹/₄ x 5⁵/₈ inches (14.3 x 33.7 cm), to cover the boards; be sure the grain runs in the direction of the spine

2 pieces of bookbinder's board or ¹/₄-inch (6 mm) hard-board, cut to 8¹/₄ x 5³/₄ inches (21 x 14.7 cm)

2 pieces card stock, cut to 8 x 6³/₄ inches (14.7 x 27.4 cm), for the end pages

1 piece of charcoal or other sturdy paper, cut as described below, for the paper case

TOOLS

Foam brush, 2 inches (5.1 cm) wide

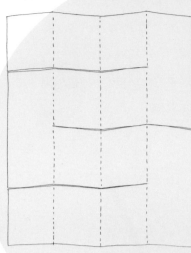

Figure 1

MAP BOOK
FIVE-MINUTE MODEL

Start with a standard-size 8½ x 11 (21.6 x 27.9 cm) sheet of copier paper. Fold it in half lengthwise. Fold each lengthwise half in half again. Repeat the procedure in the other direction, then open out the paper completely and tear along the folds, as shown in figure 1. Beginning at one corner, fold down each row accordion style as shown.

1 To better understand how the book works, first make a 5-minute model (see sidebar).

2 Cut away a 1 x 23-inch (2.5 x 58.4 cm) strip from each of the three pieces of the text paper, as shown in figure 2, then fold in the tabs.

3 Fold the text paper as you did for the 5-minute model.

4 Join the sheets of text paper by the tabs. Lay a piece of scrap paper at the base of one of the tabs, then apply glue to it (see figure 3). Remove the scrap paper, then carefully lay another piece of the text paper on top of the tab, matching the sides and edges of the sheets to each other. Burnish the paper in the overlapping areas, then lay heavy weights on the tab areas until the glue dries.

5 Cut, then refold the sheets of paper as you did for the model. The individual pages should measure 8 x 5¾ inches (14.7 x 27.4 cm).

Figure 2

Figure 4

Figure 3

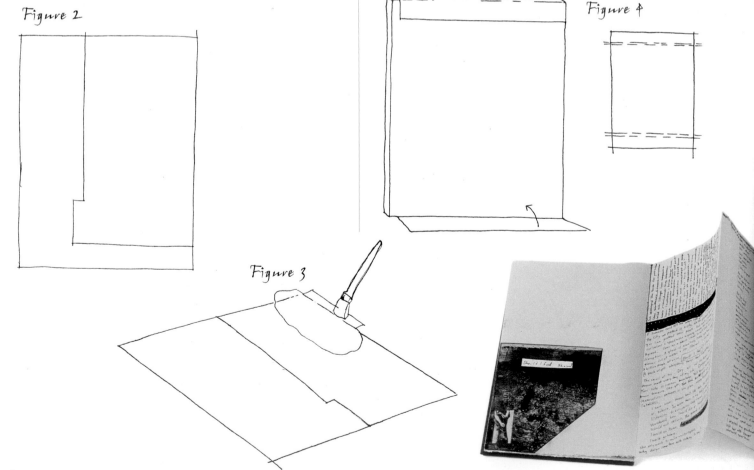

6 Lay out the piece of charcoal paper. Measure and mark a pair of score lines at each end of the paper, as shown in figure 4. Using the ruler as a guide, score the paper with the tip of the bone folder. Repeat for the second piece of charcoal paper. Fold to the inside along the scores, wrapping the paper around the board, with $^1/_8$ inch (3 mm) of the board extending out from one end of the paper.

7 Apply glue with the foam brush only to the turn-ins but not the $^1/_4$-inch (6 mm) scores, as shown in figure 5. Burnish the turn-ins to the board. Each end page of the text block will be folded into the space between the wrapper and the board. Repeat the process for the other board.

8 Unfold the text pages so they lie flat. Cut off the top left and bottom left pages as shown in figure 6. Replace these pages with the pieces of card stock, gluing them to the text paper by 1-inch (2.5 cm) tabs, as you did in step 4 (see figure 7). Slip these heavier end pages into the covers, as shown in figure 8.

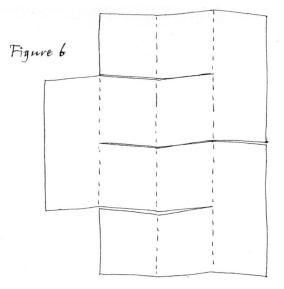

Figure 6

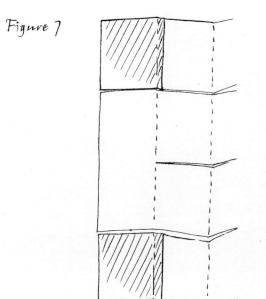

Figure 7

Figure 5

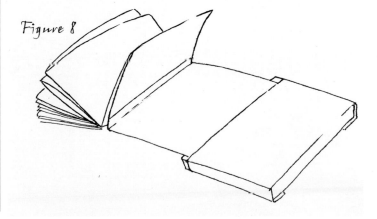

Figure 8

Making the Paper Case

1 For the paper cover, measure the height, width, and thickness of the map book. Add 5 inches to both the height and width measurements to allow for 2¹⁄₂-inch (6.4 cm) turn-ins on all sides.

2 The cover will be folded along pairs of scored lines that are ¹⁄₄ inch (6 mm) apart, as in figure 9. Lay out the piece of sturdy charcoal paper and transfer the measurements of your book to it, then score the paper with the tip of the bone folder.

3 Refer to figure 10 for the rest of the steps. Use a 45° triangle to mark the tab cuts. Cut away the corner sections along these lines, using the craft knife and the ruler.

4 Beginning with the lengthwise sides, crease the score marks, folding them all to the inside of the cover.

5 At the base of each tab, mark a dot on either side, where it rests on the turn-in.

6 Open the cover out flat, with the dots facing up, and use the ruler and craft knife to cut a slit for each tab. Fold the cover, slipping the tabs into the slits. Slip the boards into the cover's front and back openings.

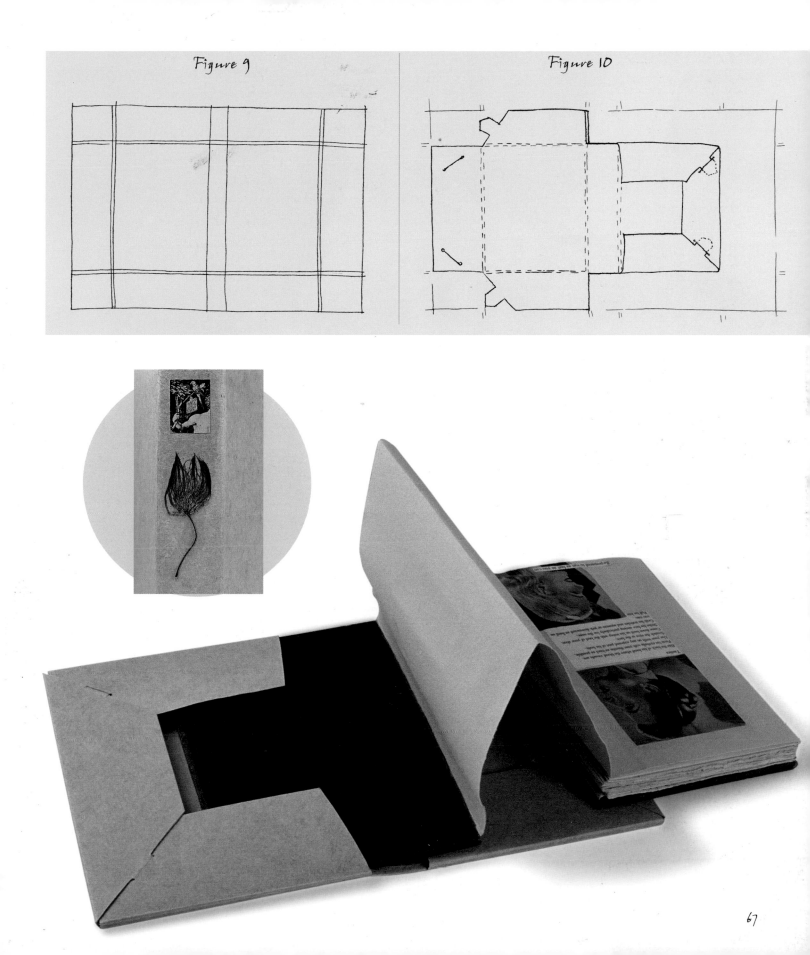

Figure 9   Figure 10

"Every artist dips his brush in his own soul, and paints his nature into his pictures." —Henry Ward Beecher

Designer:
Gwen Diehn

Journaler:
Phil Diehn

Designer's Statement: *Phil wanted a sketchbook with paper heavy enough to support watercolor without warping, and he wanted each sheet of paper interleaved with a sheet of tracing paper, so he could make notes right on top of his sketches without actually writing on them. It needed to be small and portable, but large enough to work with comfortably; sturdy, yet flexible, so he could carry it in a backpack or in his jacket pocket. I gave the 6 x 4 text block a leather wrapping, tied with a leather lace. For text pages we chose a two-ply bristol paper with a plate finish, and the tracing pages are colored glassine sheets.*

Journaler's Statement: *I prefer to work with pen and ink, watercolor, gouache, and thin-wash acrylic as media for field and travel sketches. In this book made for me, the smooth surface of the bristol paper is perfect for controlling both wet-wash techniques and drybrush drawings. The paper's heavy weight prevents buckling when wet which has often been a problem in the other sketchbooks I've used. The translucent glassine pages, placed between the pages of the white drawing paper, are useful for making field notes directly over a drawing without having to mark up the original. Typically, most of my travel sketches are line drawings, and in this journal I use the overlay to make notes about the subject as well as zone notes regarding color and value.*

PAINTER'S JOURNAL

The wraparound leather cover on this pocket-sized journal is wonderfully durable, and the text block was made from materials that are familiar to part-time painter Phil Diehn. He likes to use a particular type of smooth and heavy drawing paper, and especially warmed to the idea of using semitransparent overlays on each page, so that color notes could be made in the field, right on top of the sketches. The paint is applied at his leisure, after returning to the studio or hotel room.

FOR THE TEXT BLOCK

28 sheets of medium-weight drawing paper, cut into 6 x 9-inch (15.2 x 22.9 cm) double text pages; folded into 7 signatures

21 sheets of glassine or tracing paper, cut into 6 x 9-inch (15.2 x 22.9 cm) double text pages, 3 folios interleaved into each of the 7 signatures

Two-ply cotton bookbinder's thread

3 pieces bookbinder's tape, each 3 inches (7.6 cm) long

2 end papers, each the exact size of a folio of text paper

2 headbands, each the width of the sewn spine of the text block

Book cloth, 6 x 4 inches (15.2 11.4 cm), for the hinge

FOR THE COVER

A piece of supple leather big enough to wrap around the sewn text block three times. In the example shown, the piece of leather was 6 x 18 inches (15.2 x 45.7 cm)

Leather lace, 4 feet (1.2 m) long

1 Sew the text block of the book from the signatures, following the directions for Sewing on Tapes, as described on page 29.

2 Assemble the signatures, endpapers, headbands, and hinge, as described in Assembling the Text Block on page 30.

3 Cut the leather with a mat knife and ruler, so it is ¼ inch (6 mm) bigger than the height of the text block, and three times the width plus two times the width of the spine. See figure 1.

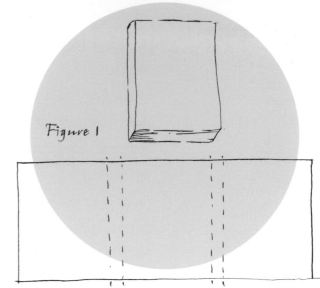

Figure 1

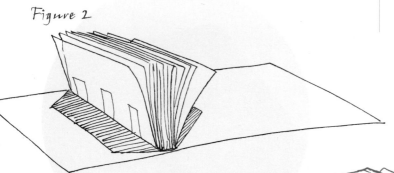

Figure 2

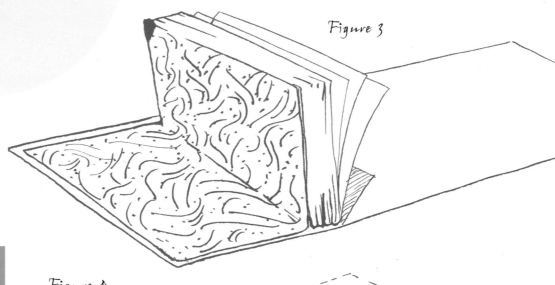

Figure 3

Figure 4

Joining the Cover to the Text Block

1 Lay the piece of leather inside out on a tabletop. Place the text block ¼ inch (6 mm) from the left edge of the leather, and use a pencil to mark the location of the spine.

2 Apply glue all over the outside of the front flap of the text block hinge. Carefully place the spine in position on the pencil marks you made. Press the gluey hinge flap to the inside of the leather, as in figure 2. Repeat this step for the other hinge flap.

3 Place a piece of scrap paper between the folds of the front piece of endpaper. Brush glue all over the outside of the front end paper, then position it so that it covers the hinge flap and the inside front cover of the book (see figure 3). Hold the text block standing upright while you press the endpaper down. Repeat this step for the back endpaper.

4 Burnish the endpapers well. Close the book and press down on it slightly. To trim the cover flap, first draw a curve on one corner of the flap. Cut the corner with scissors along the line you have drawn. Use the cut-off shape as a pattern to mark the other corner. Cut that corner to match the first one, as shown in figure 4.

Finishing the Book

1 Use a mat knife to cut two short slits in the center of the cover flap a few inches in from the rounded end (see figure 5).

2 Figure 5 shows the leather lace threaded through one hole and out the other. Pull the lace ends even, then close the book and wrap the laces around it, anchoring them by slipping them through the piece of lacing that joins the two slits.

Figure 5

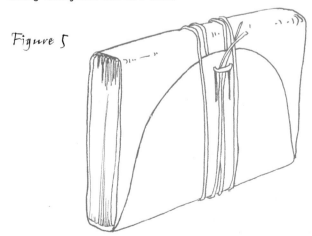

Designer:
Dan Essig

Journaler:
Priscilla Johnson

Designer's Statement: *Priscilla wanted a journal she could stuff everything into, from seed packets to her own handmade paper, so pockets were a definite design element for this book. I also selected a variety of papers for the journal so that she could find a page to accomodate every media, including, watercolors, photos, sketches, notes, and pressed leaves. The plywood covers will accept the kind of abuse an outdoor journal can expect to get, but the green paper cover (inspired by her shade garden) softens their appearance.*

Journaler's Statement:
My journal is a totally successful collaborative piece. I picked out colors, textures, images, and styles that felt close to my own nature. When I saw the finished journal, it instantly felt very familiar and as if I had loved it all along, even before it was made. Originally, I was looking for a book that I could toss around—that could handle being tossed into the back seat of the pickup, or left outdoors; I could carry it around with me to nurseries and take notes in it on the floor of the tool shed. Dan was very sensitive to my needs and desires for this journal., so, WOW, what a fantastic collaboration.

GARDENER'S JOURNAL

The weather-resistant covers of this very practical gardener's journal are subtly colored with washes of acrylic paints, then decorated with an inlaid image and curling stitches that are reminiscent of young fiddlehead ferns. Its entire spine is covered by beautiful chained, kettle, and herringbone stitches. Lively pages—some made from natural materials, some pocketed—keep pace with an active journaler: her notes, plans, even bits of the garden itself, bring journaler Priscilla Johnson's experience of the garden right onto the paper.

FOR THE TEXT BLOCK

8 sheets of heavy writing, drawing, and watercolor papers, cut into 8¹/₂ x 13-inch (21.6 x 33 cm) double text pages; folded into 4 signatures

1 sheet of 90 lb. hot press watercolor paper, 8¹/₂ x 22 inches (21.6 x 55.9 cm)

1 sheet of heavy black paper, 8¹/₂ x 22 inches (21.6 x 55.9 cm)

FOR THE COVER

Tough, heavyweight brown paper that folds well (such as charcoal or card stock), cut to 8¹/₂ x 16 inches (21.6 x 40.6 cm), for the concertina guard

2 pieces ³/₁₆-inch (4.8 mm) plywood, cut to 9 x 7 inches (22.9 x 17.8 cm) each

2 strips ³/₁₆-inch (4.8 mm) plywood, cut to 6¹/₄ x ⁵/₈ inches (15.9 cm x 1.6 mm) each

1 strip ³/₁₆-inch (4.8 mm) plywood, cut to 9 x ⁵/₈ inches (22.9 x 1.6 cm)

1 strip ³/₁₆-inch (4.8 mm) plywood, cut to 9 x 3/8 inches (22.9 cm x 9.5 mm)

2 strips ³/₁₆-inch (4.8 mm) plywood, cut to 6¹/₄ x ³/₈ inches (15.9 cm x 9.5 mm) each

2 pieces two-ply bristol board, cut to 8⁵/₈ x 6¹/₄ inches (21.9 x 15.9 cm)

Brown kraft paper or a brown paper bag for the covers, cut to 10 x 22 inches (25.4 x 55.9 cm)

Photocopy of a handwritten letter

1 piece of two-ply mat board, each cut to 5³/₄ x 8¹/₂ inches (14.6 x 21.6 cm)

Color photocopy, trimmed to 2¹/₄ x 3 inches (5.7 x 7.6 cm)

4 strips of stamped metallic foil, two strips 2¹/₄ inches (5.7 cm), and 2 strips 3 inches (7.6 cm)

1 piece of decorative paper, cut to 10 x 3 inches (25.4 x 7.6 cm), for the inside cover pockets

2 pieces of decorative paper, cut to 8¹/₂ x 6¹/₄ x inches (21.6 x 15.9 cm), for the inside cover pockets

3 small decorative buttons

SUPPLIES AND TOOLS

Yellow wood glue

4 C-clamps

Damp cloth for cleanup

Sandpaper, 125- and 220-grit

Sanding block

4 foam paint brushes, each 2 inches (5.1 cm) wide

Acrylic paint in your choice of 2 colors (brown and green were used in the example)

Matte or semi-matte spray acrylic sealer

Scrap of corrugated cardboard

Four-ply waxed linen thread, black and beige

Toothpicks

Photocopy of spiral template

Electric handheld multipurpose tool with 3mm drill bit, or a bit just slightly larger than the needle diameter

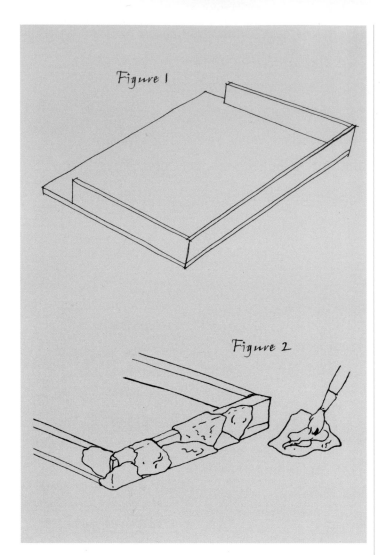

Figure 1

Figure 2

Making the Covers

1 Lay one of the cover boards flat on a work surface. Glue the ⁵⁄₈-inch (1.6 cm) strips to the top, bottom, and one long side of one of the boards, using yellow wood glue (see figure 1). Clamp them until dry. This is the front cover.

2 Repeat step 1 for the back cover, using the ³⁄₈-inch (9.5 mm) strips.

3 Use the 125-grit sandpaper on the sanding block to slightly soften and round the corners and edges of the wood pieces, so they won't wear through the cover material. Finish sanding with the 220-grit sandpaper, and wipe the covers down with a damp cloth.

4 Soften the kraft paper by crumpling it, so it easily conforms to the edges of the covers. Tear pieces of the paper, then use a foam brush to coat them with PVA, as shown in figure 2. Apply the torn paper randomly to the covers, as you would papier maché, making sure the edges overlap and cover the wood completely. Continue the gluing around to the inside lips of the covers, burnishing the covers well when you're finished. Dry under a heavy weight.

5 Once the glued paper has dried, paint the cover with green acrylic paint.

6 Photocopy a handwritten letter, then glue it to the 5³⁄₄ x 8¹⁄₂ inch (14.6 x 21.6 cm) piece of mat board with PVA. Burnish with a bone folder so the paper is very smooth. Using a craft knife and the ruler, trim the excess photocopy paper to the edges of the mat board.

7 For a mottled effect, use a crumpled paper towel to apply the brown acrylic paint to the photocopied letter and the edges of the mat board. Slip the board inside a folio of wax paper and put under a heavy weight until thoroughly dry.

8 To assemble the decorative piece for the front cover, first glue the color photocopy to the mounted letter, slightly above the exact center, and burnish it well. Glue the strips of stamped metallic foil onto the edges of the color photocopy. Now glue the decorative piece onto the cover 1 inch (2.5 cm) in from the left (spine) edge and ¹⁄₄ inch (6 mm) away from the head, tail, and fore edge. Lay a piece of wax paper over the cover, and put under a weight until dry.

9 Apply two or more coats of spray sealer to the outsides of the covers.

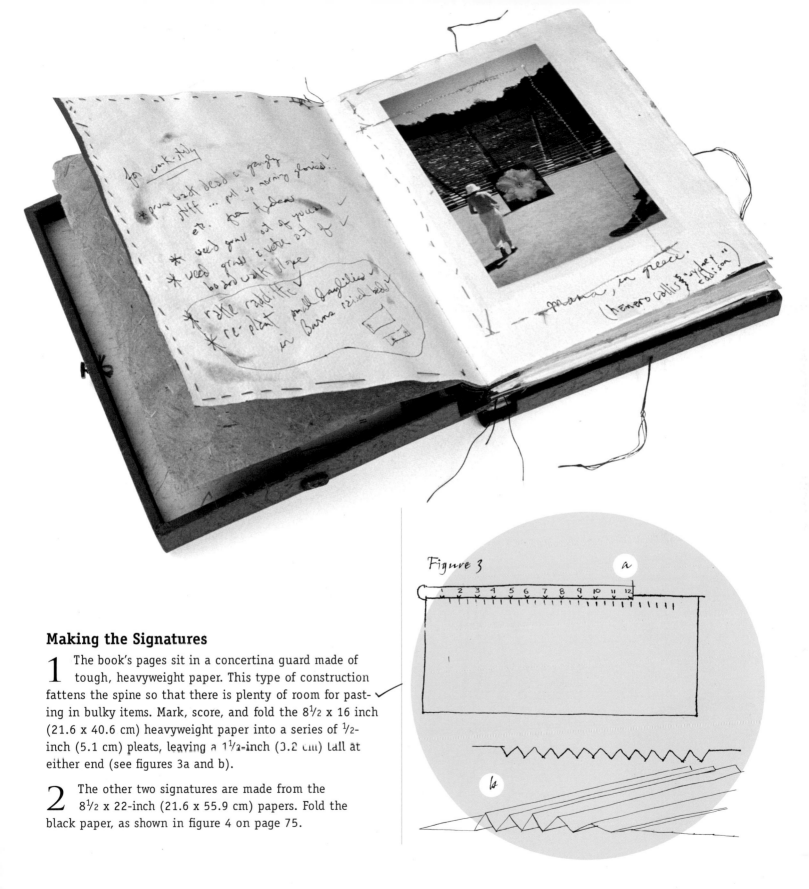

Making the Signatures

1 The book's pages sit in a concertina guard made of tough, heavyweight paper. This type of construction fattens the spine so that there is plenty of room for pasting in bulky items. Mark, score, and fold the 8$\frac{1}{2}$ x 16 inch (21.6 x 40.6 cm) heavyweight paper into a series of $\frac{1}{2}$-inch (5.1 cm) pleats, leaving a 1$\frac{1}{2}$-inch (3.2 cm) tail at either end (see figures 3a and b).

2 The other two signatures are made from the 8$\frac{1}{2}$ x 22-inch (21.6 x 55.9 cm) papers. Fold the black paper, as shown in figure 4 on page 75.

Figure 3

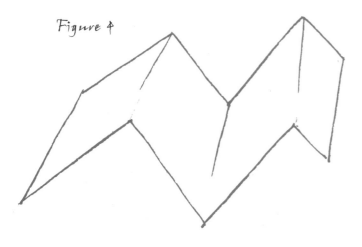

Figure 4

3 Photocopy the template (figure 5) for the pattern of sewing holes. Fold the template lengthwise along the line of marks, then lay it into the signature fold and mark the holes.

4 Nest the first signature into the concertina. Refer to figure 6 to see the order in which the folios fit into the concertina. Use an awl to pierce through the template, the signature, and the concertina for each signature, as shown in figure 7. Repeat for the other signatures.

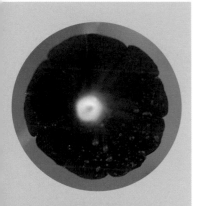

Figure 5

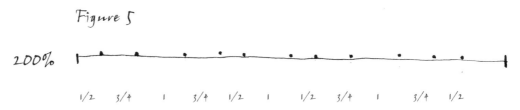

200%

1/2   3/4   1   3/4   1/2   1   1/2   3/4   1   3/4   1/2

Figure 6

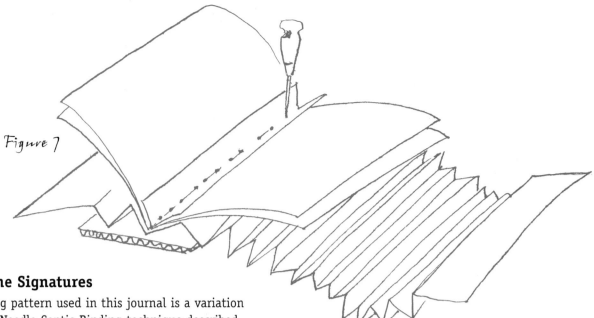

Figure 7

Sewing the Signatures

The stitching pattern used in this journal is a variation on the One-Needle Coptic Binding technique described on page 32.

1 Begin with one signature on one end of the concertina; you will add the others, one at a time, during the sewing process. Thread the needle with a length of beige waxed linen thread. Follow the sewing pattern as shown in figure 8. At the fourth and seventh stations, loop the thread around a toothpick before reinserting the needle back into the same hole. The toothpick holds the loop open until it is caught by the next pass of the needle in the concertina above it.

2 Bring the needle up and into the end hole of the next concertina. As you sew along this empty fold, you will be picking up stitches from the first signature to create the herringbone stitches (figures 9a and b). For the chained stitch, remove the toothpick from the first concertina, and pass the needle up through the bottom of the loop it left (figure 10 on page 78); use a toothpick again in the new stitch, to maintain an open loop.

3 When you reach the tail, pull the thread taut in the direction parallel to the spine; this will close up any loose stitches, including the looped ones. Leaving the needle on the thread, tie a square knot with the thread end from the first signature.

4 At the end of the third concertina fold (the second signature of paper is inside it), make a kettle stitch (see figure 11 on page 78). Finish sewing up and down the concertina folds and signatures, ending each one with a kettle stitch. If, during your sewing, you run short of thread on the needle, join it to a new length of thread with a weaver's knot on the inside of a signature where it won't show.

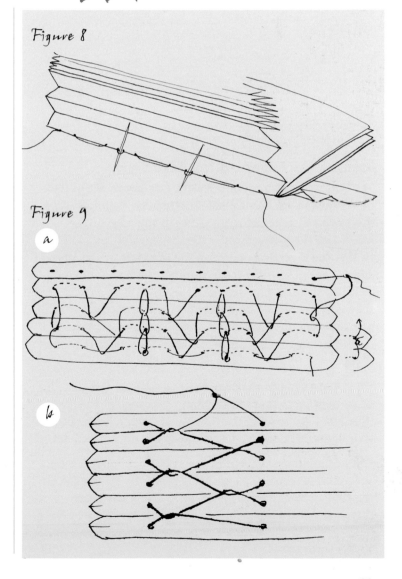

Figure 8

Figure 9

a

b

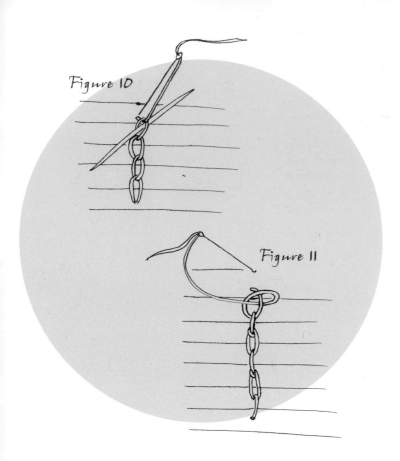

Figure 10

Figure 11

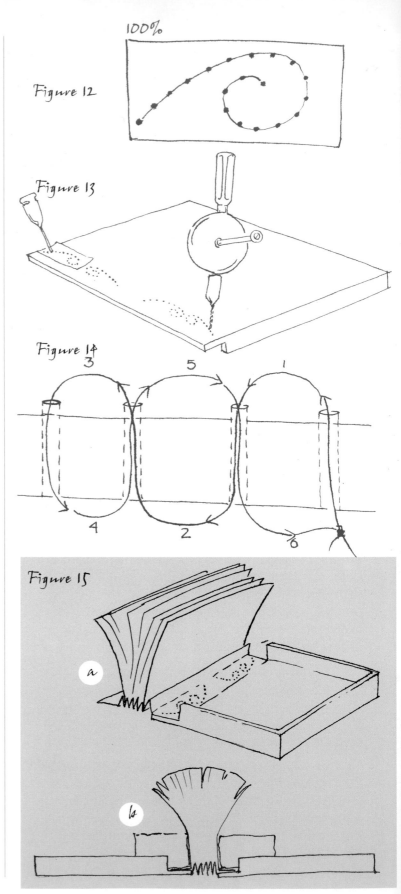

100%

Figure 12

Figure 13

Figure 14

Figure 15

Joining the Covers to the Text Block

1 Photocopy the spiral template (see figure 12; in the example, each spiral has 19 stitches), then trim it to the same width as the space between the edge of the board and the photocopied letter. To transfer the pattern to the wood, correctly position the template at the spine edge of the cover, then poke through the holes with an awl. Use the drill to make the holes in both covers, as shown in figure 13. Use a pamphlet stitch (figure 14) to sew the pattern of holes with the black linen thread, beginning and ending on the insides. Repeat for the other cover.

2 Apply glue to the 1½-inch (3.2 cm) concertina tails, then press these to the flat, open edge of the covers. Use the bricks to keep the text block standing straight up (see figures 15a and b). Leave under the bricks until dry.

3 To reinforce the join of the text block to the covers, drill 17 evenly-spaced holes along the spine edge of the covers. Sew through these holes, using the beige thread and a reinforcing pamphlet stitch (see figure 16). Begin and end the sewing on the inside of the cover; finish with a square knot.

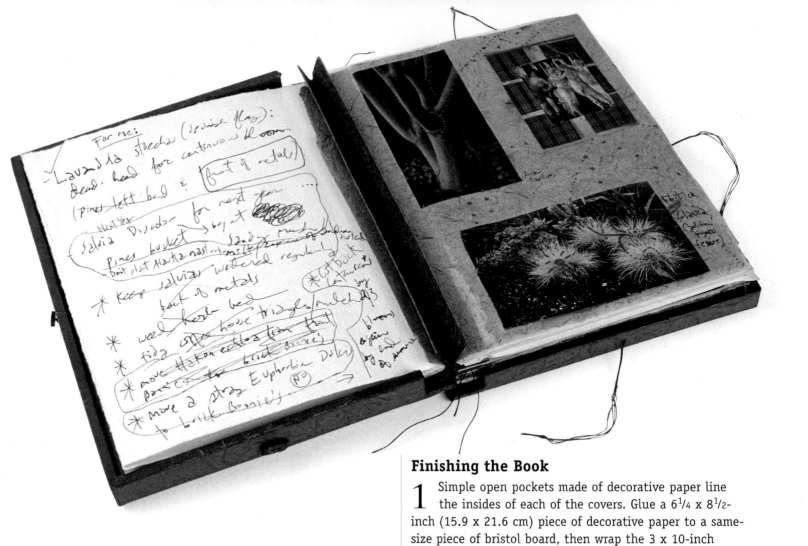

Finishing the Book

1 Simple open pockets made of decorative paper line the insides of each of the covers. Glue a 6¹/₄ x 8¹/₂-inch (15.9 x 21.6 cm) piece of decorative paper to a same-size piece of bristol board, then wrap the 3 x 10-inch (7.6 x 25.4 cm) piece of paper around it to make the pocket, as shown in figures 17a and b).

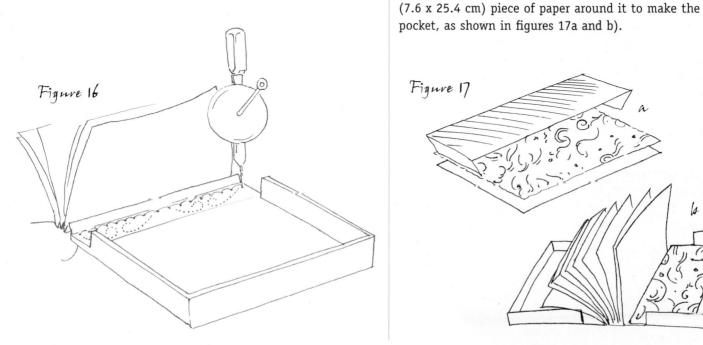

Figure 16

Figure 17

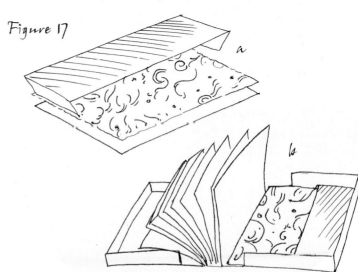

a

b

2 Apply PVA with a foam brush to the back side of the liner, then press it onto the inside of one of the covers. Dry under a heavy weight. Repeat for the other cover.

3 Drill a hole in the center and ¹/₂ inch (1.3 cm) in from each of the fore edges of the covers for the closures (figure 18). Use the brown thread to sew a button to each side of the front cover; finish with a double knot on the inside, as shown in figure 19.

4 Cut three 6-inch (15.2 cm) pieces of brown thread, and tie a double knot near one end of each piece. Pass a length of thread through one of the holes in the bottom cover and tie a double knot close to the wood. Tie another double knot 3 inches (7.6 cm) away, and snip off the excess thread with scissors. Repeat for the other two holes in the bottom cover. Wrap the thread around the buttons to close the covers.

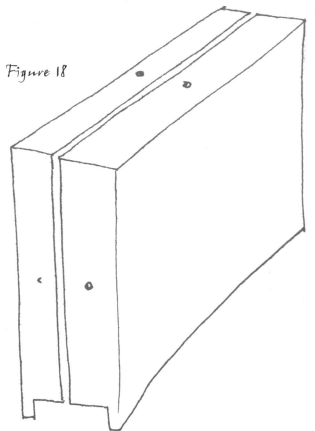

Figure 18

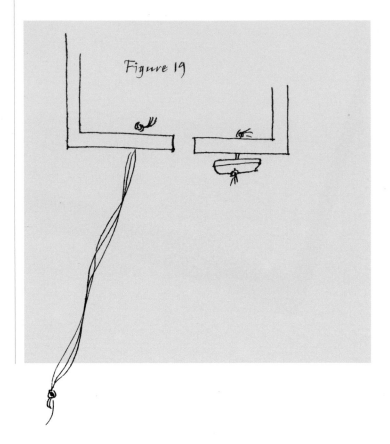

Figure 19

No bird, but an invisible thing, A voice, a mystery. —William Wordsworth

Designer:
Dan Essig

Journaler:
Susan Katz

Designer's Statement: *Susan wanted a book that would inspire her to journal about her favorite subject. She asked for a toothy watercolor paper that would allow her to express her thoughts with ink, paint, and collage.*

Journaler's Statement: *Using this journal has helped me to express myself in a way I don't often explore. Having beautiful paper and materials to write and paint on is inspirational. The shape of the book and its birdlike characteristics help me focus on my subject.*

BIRD LOVER'S JOURNAL

The shape of this unusual journal continually reminds the journaler to explore her fascination with bird shapes, bird behavior, and bird lore. The soft leather "wings" open to reveal a top spine text block that lets Susan's drawing and writing flow freely across the page. Inside the back cover of this wood, leather, and paper book is a neat little feather holder, for treasured finds.

FOR THE TEXT BLOCK

18 sheets of 90-lb. cream watercolor paper cut to 8⅞ x 9½-inch (22.5 x 24.1 cm) double text pages; folded into 6 signatures

FOR THE COVER

Brown charcoal or other sturdy paper, cut to 14½ x 9 inches (36.8 x 22.9 cm), for the text block wrapper

3 pieces of brown charcoal or other sturdy paper, cut to 14½ x 9 inches (36.8 x 22.9 cm); ¼ x 12 inches (6 mm x 30.5 cm); and 1 x 9 inches (2.5 x 22.9 cm)

Wood board, cut to ⅜ x 9⅛ x 5 inches (9.5 mm x 23.2 x 12.7 cm); in the example, a piece of sycamore was used, but any sturdy wood may be substituted

2 pieces of thin, supple leather, 5 x 13⁹⁄₁₆ inches (12.7 x 34.4 cm) each, cut as described below, for the wing shapes

1 piece of thin, supple leather, 3 x 3 inches (7.6 x 7.6 cm), cut as described below, for the tail

2 pieces of brown charcoal or other sturdy paper, 6 x 5 inches (15.2 x 12.7 cm), cut as described below, for the wing liner pieces

SUPPLIES AND TOOLS

3 pieces of 8½ x 14-inch (21.6 x 35.6) card stock for the photocopies of the wing and tail templates

Clean cotton rag

Paste wax

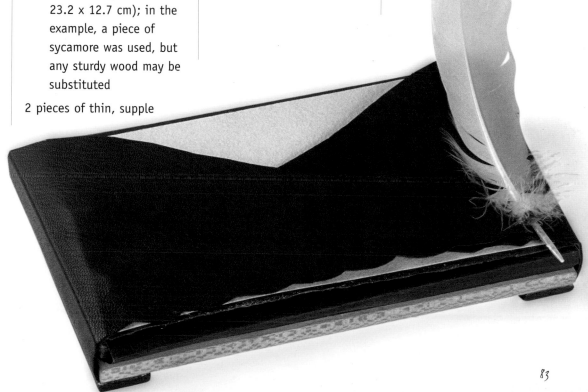

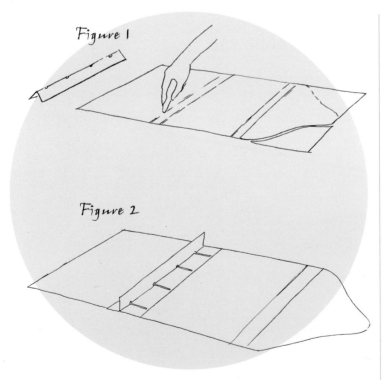

Figure 1

Figure 2

1 Score and fold the 14½ x 9-inch (36.8 x 22.9 cm) piece of paper, as shown in figure 1, then cut out the curving piece where the "tail" will be glued. This is the text block wrapper.

2 Fold a piece of scrap paper in half lengthwise, and use it to measure and mark four holes along the inside of the fold, beginning and ending ½ inch (1.3 cm) from each end. Save the template for marking the wrapper in the next section.

Sewing the Signatures

1 Assemble the signatures you made from the watercolor paper. Use the template to mark the sewing holes and also to mark the placement of the crosswise slits in the ⅝-inch (1.6 cm) area of the wrapper's spine, as shown in figure 2. The slits should match exactly with the stations in the signatures. Cut the slits in the wrapper with a craft knife.

2 Put the first signature inside the wrapper, lining up the stations with the slits in the wrapper. Thread the

needle with the waxed thread and sew the signatures together, one at a time, following the pattern shown in figure 3. Finish the sewing on the inside of the last signature, using a half-hitch knot (see figure 4).

Making the Cover

1 Use the two strips of charcoal paper to make the feather holder. With a craft knife, cut slots in the 12-inch (30.5 cm) strip, as shown in figure 5. Weave the 9-inch (22.9 cm) strip in and out of the slots. Trim the feather holder to 7³/₄ inches (19.8 cm) in length, then glue down the tails with dabs of PVA.

2 Apply glue to the back of the holder, then adhere it to the inside back cover of the wrapper (see figure 6). Use the tip of the bone folder to press down the bottom strip without creasing the loops.

3 Apply glue to the back of the wrapper, then adhere it to the piece of wood, pressing the paper firmly and smoothly to the wood with your fingers. Put under a heavy weight overnight until thoroughly dry.

Figure 3
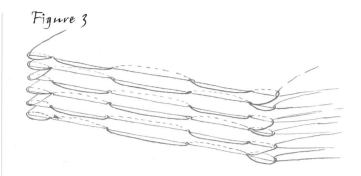

Figure 4
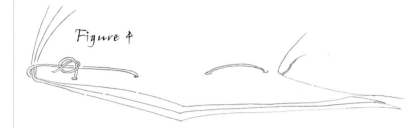

Figure 5
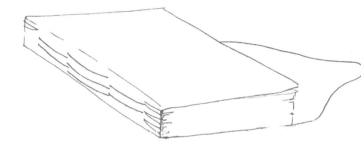

Figure 6

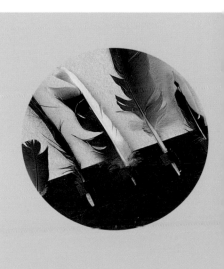

Figure 7

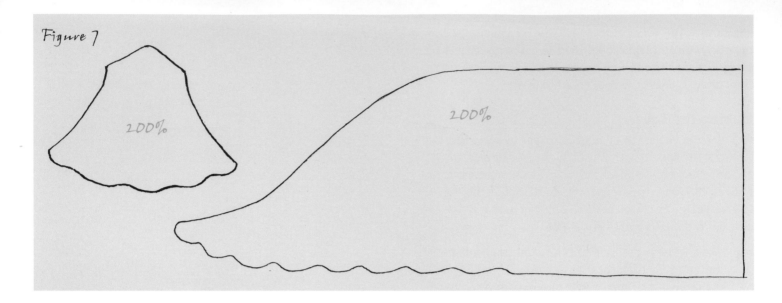

200%

200%

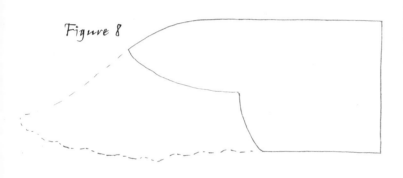

Figure 8

4 Photocopy the wing and tail templates (figure 7) onto card stock, and cut them out with scissors. Transfer the wing and tail shapes onto the leather pieces, then cut out them out with scissors.

5 Draw and cut out a new shape from the wing template, as shown in figure 8. Use this new shape to cut out two liners from the two 6 x 5-inch (15.2 x 12.7 cm) pieces of brown charcoal paper.

6 Adhere these liners to the inside of the leather wings with glue (figure 9). Lay out the wings, liner side up, and cover them with sheets of wax paper; dry under weights. Attach the tail to the curved (fore edge) end of the wrapper (figure 10), and dry it under weight.

Figure 9

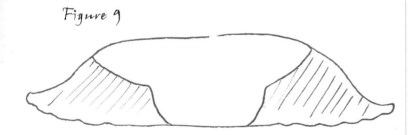

Figure 10

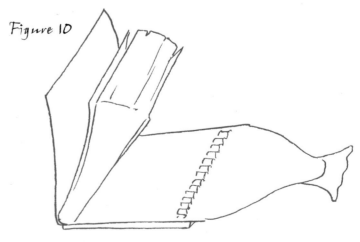

7 Use the tip of the bone folder to carefully score the wings' liner papers only, so they will fold around the text block, as shown in figure 11.

8 Seal the wood with paste wax.

9 Adhere the wings to the back cover board; their straight sides should meet in the center of the back, the scored liners allowing them to wrap neatly around the sides of the text block. Put under a heavy weight until dry.

10 For the front cover closure, shape a strip of $\frac{1}{4}$ x $\frac{3}{4}$-inch (6 x 19 mm) charcoal paper over the quill of a large feather. Glue the ends of the loop near the fold in the right wing (see figure 12).

11 Cut a small rectangular hole in the tip of the left wing where it overlaps the loop on the right wing. Use the feather to hold the covers closed, as shown in figure 13.

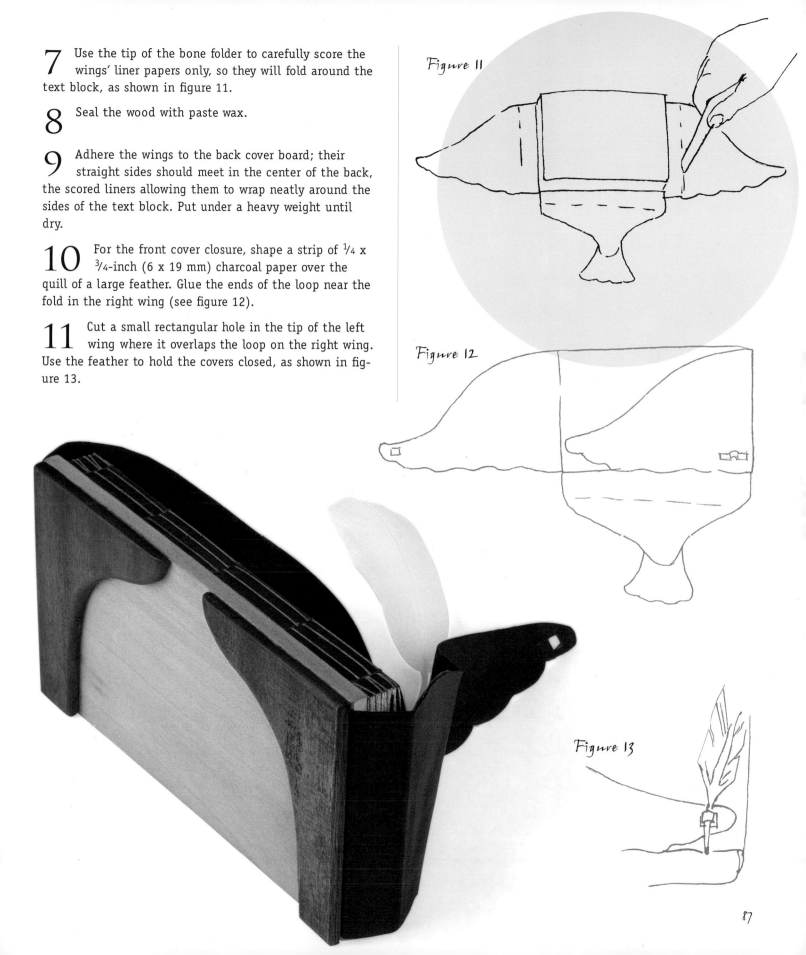

Figure 11

Figure 12

Figure 13

Designer:
Coral Jensen

Journaler:
Kate Mathews

Designer's Statement: *Kate has filled her journal with ideas for her Cowgirl Quilts. Working with design and layout, she prefers graph paper with a tight grid. Overleaves of tracing vellum allow her to play and layer the design on the page without the grid becoming a part of the design. Because she uses so many different materials, colors, and embellishments, I thought it appropriate to add envelopes for her stashes of quilt swatches.*

Journaler's Statement: *Working with grid paper to plan pieced quilts makes perfect sense, so I appreciate Coral's facing every grid page with vellum. I can see it clearly while drawing piecework ideas, then I can put a piece of plain paper behind the vellum page to block out the grid and see the design alone. The built-in envelopes are great for stashing fabric samples. They save me the time it takes to go back to the studio to look for swatches. I'd sit down to draw, and within 15 minutes I'd want to go straight to the sewing machine. Drawing out ideas in pencil is very helpful for me, distilling my thoughts and images into a design concept. I never thought a journal could be such a motivator!*

QUILTER'S JOURNAL

Quilters are planners and dreamers: they must dream the design, then carry out their vision with precision and careful planning. Each gridded page is overlaid with a vellum sheet, so that journaler Kate Mathews can separate her drawings from the graph paper underneath it when she wants to check on the progress of her design. Kate's interest in the lore of early women cowpunchers, sharpshooters, and horse thieves is evoked in the "branded" leather cover, closed with a ponytail-braided lash and Southwestern turquoise bead.

FOR THE TEXT BLOCK

32 sheets of 1/4-inch (6 mm) nonreproduction blue graph paper (available at architectural supply stores), cut to 6 x 18-inch (15.2 x 45.7 cm) double text pages, and folded into 16 signatures

32 sheets of tracing vellum, cut to 6 x 18-inch (15.2 x 45.7 cm) double text pages; interleave these with the graph paper folios

6 x 9-inch (15.2 x 22.9 cm) manila envelope, to use as a pattern

4 sheets of 13 x 15-inch (33 x 38.1 cm) decorative papers for envelopes, cut as described below

20 pieces of charcoal or other sturdy paper, cut to 2 x 6 inches (5.1 x 15.2 cm), for the spine fatteners

FOR THE COVER

2 pieces of thin, supple leather, 1/8 inch (3 mm) thick, cut to 6 x 10 inches (15.2 x 25.4 cm) and 6 x 16 inches (15.2 x 40.6 cm) each

2 strips of hardwood veneer 1/8 x 1 x 6 1/4 inches (3 mm x 2.5 x 15.9 cm)

Leather cording

Flat-sided beads

Donut bead or a disc with a hole in it

SUPPLIES AND TOOLS

Coarse sandpaper

Woodburning tool

Fine point felt-tip marker

Handheld electric multipurpose tool with 1/16-inch (1.6 mm) drill bit

Plastic triangle

Hands to work, hearts to God.

Amish adage

Figure 1

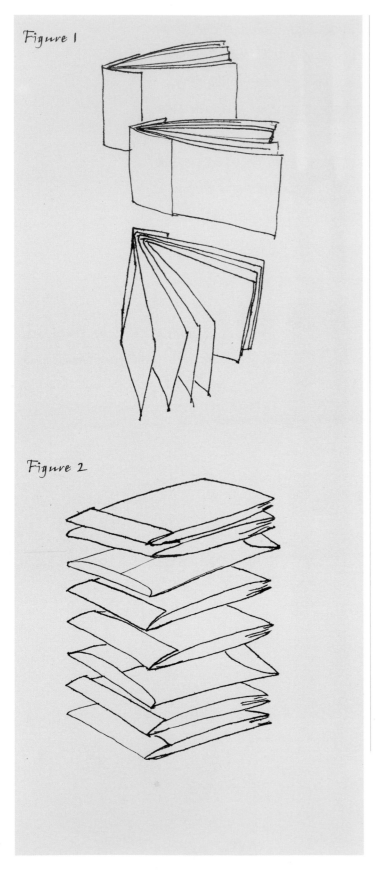

Note: This book contains 16 folio signatures and four sewn-in envelopes, for a total of 20 signatures. One-half of the signatures are sewn together at a time, then the two are braided together through the exposed stitching for each signature.

1 Take apart the 6 x 9-inch (15.2 x 22.9 cm) manila envelope, using a bone folder to separate the glued seams. Lay a sheet of the decorative paper on a clean surface, and use a pencil to trace the envelope's outline, marking the fold lines onto it. Cut it out. Fold the correct creases into the envelope, but don't apply any glue yet. Repeat for the other three pieces of decorative paper.

2 Fold the 2 x 6-inch (5.1 x 15.2 cm) strips in half lengthwise. Apply glue to the inner side of the strips, then adhere them to the outermost folio in each signature, as shown in figure 1.

3 Stack the signatures with a layer of wax paper between each one. Put the text block in a press, or under heavy weights, until thoroughly dry.

Figure 2

4 Make two stacks of eight signatures each, and insert two folded envelopes between the second and third signatures, and the fourth and fifth, in each stack, so that their bottom folds are at the spine edge, aligned evenly with the folds of the folios. See figure 2.

Making the Cover

1 To make the back cover, trim one end of the larger leather piece into a rounded triangle, as shown in figure 3. Use the sandpaper to give the leather a weathered and aged look. Use the woodburning tool to create symbols and words on the leather pieces. Repeat this process for the front cover piece.

2 Punch two holes 1¹⁄₂ inches (3.8 cm) apart, at the triangular end of the back cover. If you do not have a leather punch, ask a shoe repair shop to do it for you.

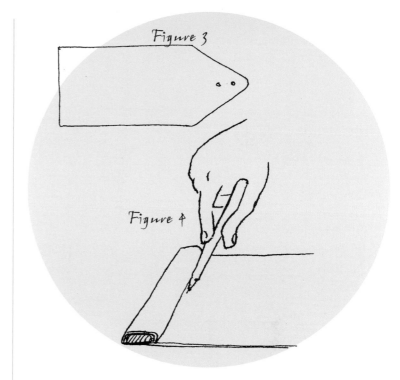

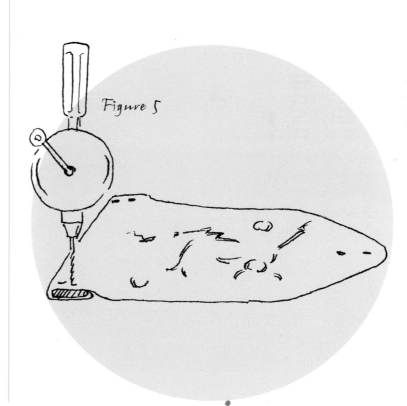

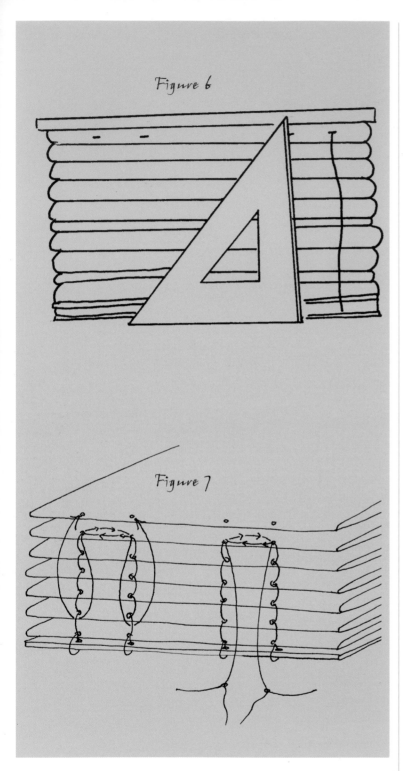

Figure 6

Figure 7

3 Lay one of the veneer strips at the spine edge of one of the leather pieces. Roll the strip and the leather over, and use a felt-tip marker to mark the leather along the side of the veneer strip (see figure 4 on page 91). Apply craft glue liberally to the leather, from the spine edge up to the mark you made. Lay the strip of veneer on the glued edge, and wrap the rest of the glued leather to the wood. Repeat for the other piece of leather. Firmly press all the surfaces and let dry.

4 Drill a pair of holes through the leather-covered veneer strips, ³⁄₄ inch (1.9 cm) in from the head and tail of the front and back covers, as shown in figure 5, on page 91. These holes are for the sewn-in headbands. The drill bit should be slightly larger than the needle you'll be sewing with. In the example, a ¹⁄₁₆-inch (1.6 mm) bit and a 1 mm needle were used.

Marking the Text Block for Sewing

1 The text block is ¹⁄₄ inch (6 mm) shorter than the leather covers. Make a template from a scrap piece of paper measuring the height of the covers, and mark the template ¹⁄₈ inch (3 mm) in from the head and tail, so the block will be centered between the head and tail of the covers. For the four-needle Coptic binding style shown here, mark the template with the location of four evenly spaced stations.

2 Put two pieces of scrap board on either side of the block, then put the block in a vise with the spine exposed. Use the template to mark the position of the sewing holes on an outermost signature, then use a triangle to extend these marks across the spine (see figure 6).

3 Use the awl to pierce the signatures at the marks you made.

Sewing the Text Blocks

Note: Complete the stitching in each signature before adding the next one. The directions are given for one pair of needles; repeat the stitch for the second pair before going on to the next signature.

1 Thread two needles at the ends of a length of thread, then do the same with another piece of thread.

2 Sew the cover and the first five signatures together, using the Two-Needle Coptic binding method described on page 33.

3   After crossing over and exiting the needles on the
    sixth signature, drop the needles down and pass
them behind the stitches that lie between the first and
second signature (figure 7). Bring the needles back up and
add the seventh signature, then again drop the needles
down, this time behind the second and third signatures.
Continue this pattern as you sew the rest of the signatures
together. End with the needles outside the last signature.

4   Sew the other stack of signatures together, as you
    did in steps 1 through 3.

5   In order to join the two text blocks, first stack them
    on top of each other. All the needles should be out-
side the two text blocks. Referring to figure 8, bring each
pair of needles up from the bottom block, and enter them
into the corresponding holes on the first signature of the
top block. Cross the needles over one another on the
inside of the signature, as before, then pass them back
through the station holes, bringing the needles once again
to the outside. Repeat this step for the pairs of needles
that sewed the top block. Now the needles from the bottom block have moved to the top block and vice versa.

6   Loop the needles behind the stitches between the
    fifth and sixth signatures, as shown in figure 9; con-
tinue to wrap thread around the stitches in this way until
the needles meet at the midpoint between the two text
blocks. This is the same procedure you used when you
added the second half of the total number of signatures to
each block.

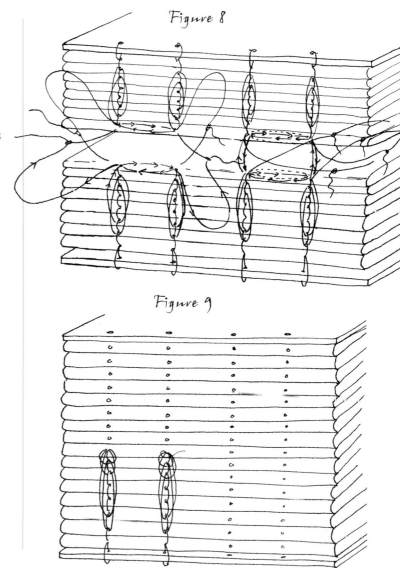

Figure 8

Figure 9

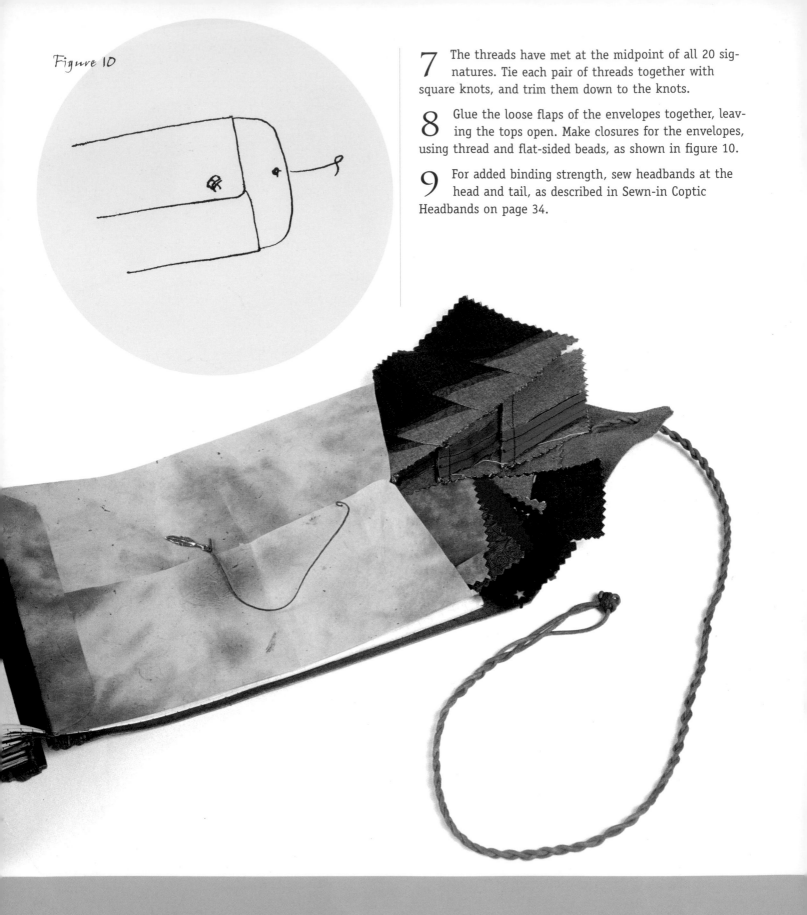

Figure 10

7 The threads have met at the midpoint of all 20 signatures. Tie each pair of threads together with square knots, and trim them down to the knots.

8 Glue the loose flaps of the envelopes together, leaving the tops open. Make closures for the envelopes, using thread and flat-sided beads, as shown in figure 10.

9 For added binding strength, sew headbands at the head and tail, as described in Sewn-in Coptic Headbands on page 34.

Making the Cover Closure

1 Braid the three lengths of leather cord together. Knot one end and thread it from the outside, through the inner hole in the back cover flap. Thread the donut bead onto the braid, then pass the braid through the outermost hole in the flap. Wrap the length of braid around the entire width of the book.

2 At the point where the braid reaches the donut bead, separate one of the cords slightly, so it forms a loop for the donut bead. Thread a smaller bead onto the braid, then knot the end. Trim the ends close to the bead.

No language, but the language of the heart.

Alexander Pope

Designer:
Dan Essig

Journaler:
Suzanne Nicaud

Designer's Statement: *I decided to make this journal palm sized to reflect the intimate nature of its purpose, and also to fit the gloves Suzanne wanted to incorporate into the cover. Rather than cutting apart the gloves, I chose to preserve their integrity and the delicate worn features they displayed by cutting the cover boards to fit inside them (the final fit was a matter of trial and error). The journal is filled with hotpress watercolor paper so that the writing would feel smooth to the hand and also support other media.*

Journaler's Statement: *This pair of worn gloves seems to hold a small treasure and suggest memories and the passing of time. I painted abstract color fields prior to and after making journal entries; the colors seem to intensify the writing experience. I also covered some of the pages' corners with bits of colored foil. The tiny Victorian paper mats that make up the shared center board were perfect for two matched photos of my brother and me.*

REUNION JOURNAL

This dos à dos (back to back) book is actually two Coptic-bound books that share a center cover. It's an ideal structure for writing about any before-and-after event. The pages were painted with watercolor paints, then additional elements were glued in. Because the journaler used waterproof ink, she can continue to add water media over the writing. The spacers between the pages allow for the addition of bulky items.

FOR THE TEXT BLOCK

30 pieces of 90 lb. hot press watercolor paper, cut to $4^7/_8$ x $6^3/_4$-inch (12.4 x 17.2 cm) double text pages, and folded into 10 signatures (5 for each side)

2 pieces of 300 lb. (136.2 kg) watercolor paper, cut to 5 x $4^7/_8$ inches (12.7 x 12.4 cm) each, for the endpapers

FOR THE COVERS

2 pieces of wood, cut to 5 x $3^1/_2$ x $3/_8$ inches (12.7 x 8.9 cm x 9.5 mm), or you can substitute book-binder's board, or laminate two thinner pieces of wood together

2 pieces of cover material (in this example, a pair of unlined leather gloves), to fit the cover

1 piece of 300 lb. (136.2 kg) watercolor paper, cut to $4^7/_8$ x $12^1/_8$ inches (12.4 x 30.8 cm), for the center cover

SUPPLIES AND TOOLS

Sandpaper, 125- and 220-grit

Electric handheld drill with a $1/_8$-inch (3 mm) drill bit, or a bit just slightly larger than the needle's diameter

Curved needles

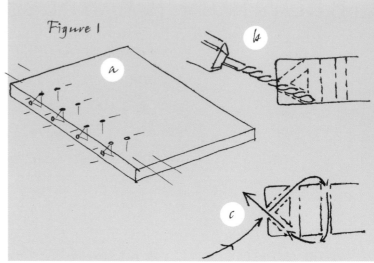

1 Use 125- and 220-grit sandpaper to sand the edges and corners, to reduce wear on the cover material. In the example, the covers were cut to fit snugly into the gloves.

2 Mark a pattern of evenly spaced holes into the spine edge cover, as shown in figure 1a. Drill these angled and straight sewing holes according to figure 1b. The sewing pattern is illustrated in figure 1c.

3 Measure and mark the two endpapers along one side (see figure 2a), so that the flaps or tails measure 1 $^1/_8$ inches (2.8 cm). Score along these lines with a bone folder, as shown in figure 2b.

4 Mark a scrap of paper with a single line of sewing holes that align perfectly with the holes in the covers; see figures 3a and b. Fold it lengthwise, and use an awl to drill the sewing holes in the folds of the signatures and all the folds in the two endpapers.

5 Cut out two small window openings in the largest piece of watercolor paper, as shown in figure 4.

Figure 2

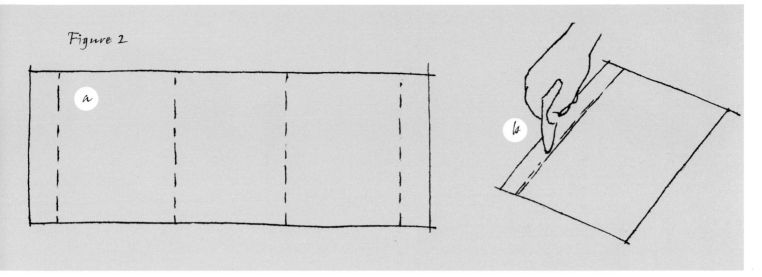

Figure 3

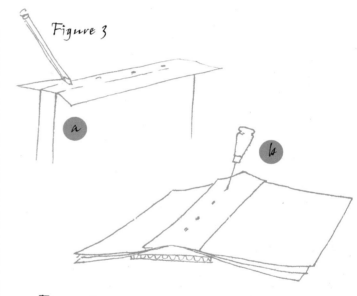

6 Fold the center cover paper into a Z shape, so there are two 1-inch (2.5 cm) flaps extending from each side of the center cover (see figure 5). Pierce sewing holes that exactly match those you pierced in the signatures into the flap folds. Pierce a decorative pattern of sewing holes into the front and back of the center cover, as shown.

7 Sew through all the folded pages of the center cover, using a pamphlet stitch (see figure 6 on page 100). Tie the ends with a square knot, as in figure 7.

Figure 4

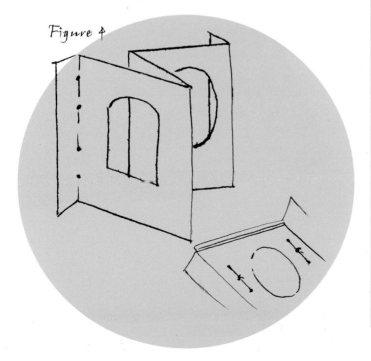

Figure 5

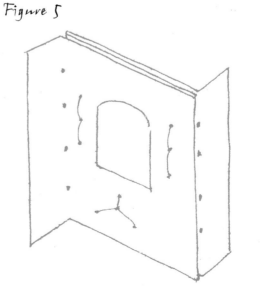

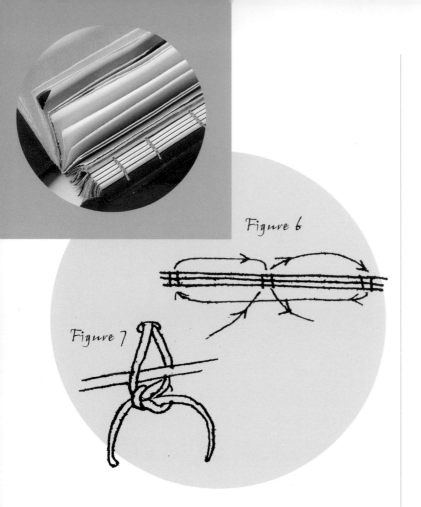

Figure 6

Figure 7

Sewing the Text Block

1 Slip the gloves or other cover material over the cover boards (figure 8). As you stitch, the sewing needles will pierce the cover material over the holes you drilled in the covers.

2 Thread two needles on a length of linen thread. Nest the first signature into the folded endpaper. Starting from the outside of the cover, follow the directions given for the Two-Needle Coptic binding method on page 33. Sew five of the signatures together for this side of the journal. Sew the center cover to the text block, as shown in figure 9.

3 Now add the first signature (with the endpaper as the outermost folio) to the other flap of the center cover. This set of signatures faces in the direction opposite that of the first book. Finish sewing the other four signatures to the text block. Add the other endpaper as you did on the other side. After adding the other outside cover, re-enter the holes in the endpaper that is next to it, then knot the threads with square knots.

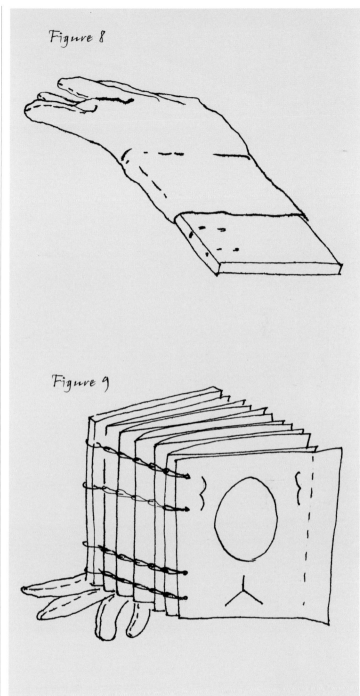

Figure 8

Figure 9

Designer:
Dan Essig

Journaler:
Amy Cook

Designer's Statement: *Amy had several personal items that were used in the book's design: her mother's hair ribbon became a bookmark; a swimmer's nose-plug acts as a closure for the covers; and a handy city map was sewn into a signature of the piggyback book that sits in the back cover's window. This smaller book is made from one piece of accordion-folded paper and a removeable paper cover; it is perfect for phone numbers and addresses and is an option to carrying around the entire journal. Because this journal was going to travel and had the potential to get buried between moving boxes, I designed it with plywood covers to withstand some abuse.*

Journaler's Statement: *When I handed over a manila envelope filled with sentimentalities (ribbon, images, knick-knacks, and gew-gaws) from my life on the East Coast, I had no idea that they would come back to me so transfigured...as WORKING parts of the book! I had no idea how much more precious that junk would feel when I stepped off the plane in San Francisco. I could just turn the pages and find traces of my roots throughout the book. I loved the way Dan included the types of paper that I needed most: smooth sheets for writing, bristol board for mixed media work, lined ledger pages for budget tracking, and more. He also sized it all extra-large, because I like a nice big surface. But tucked away in the back, peering out the back window, he secured a tiny accordian "piggyback" book for me to take with me, wherever I go.*

RELOCATION JOURNAL

Journaler Amy Cook chronicled a big move from the East to the West Coast. Some personal items that she wanted to take with her were included in the book's design: her mother's hair ribbon became a bookmark, and a swimmer's noseplug acts as a closure for the covers. Just as journeys often present us with the unexpected, this journal holds delightful combinations of different papers, odd page shapes, and stitching that spells out words on the cover. A handy little piggyback book sits in the back cover's window.

FOR THE TEXT BLOCKS

33 sheets of paper, cut to 11 x 17-inch (27.9 x 43.2 cm) double text pages; in the example, various combinations of cream watercolor papers, buff printmaker's paper, dark blue and black charcoal papers, medium weight drawing paper, and textured handmade papers were used. Some of the pages were cut into other shapes and sizes, as described below. Some of the 13 signatures have more pages in them than others.

1 piece of 80 lb. text paper, cut to $4^3/8$ x 20 inches (11.1 x 50.8 cm), then folded, accordion style, into a page size that measure $4^3/8$ x $2^1/2$ inches (11.1 x 6.4 cm), for the piggyback book

Afoot and light-hearted
I take to the open road,
Healthy, free, the world before me,
The long brown path before me leading wherever I choose.
—Walt Whitman

FOR THE COVERS

2 pieces $3/16$-inch (4.8 mm) plywood, cut to 8 x 11 inches (27.9 x 20.3 cm) each, for the cover boards

2 pieces 10 x 14-inch (25.4 x 35.6 cm) brown kraft paper

2 pieces 8 x 11 inches (20.3 x 27.9 cm) maple veneer or charcoal paper, for the covers' liners

Yellow wood glue

Map or other paper item for front cover inlay

2 pieces heavy polyester film, cut to 5 x 3 inches (12.7 x 7.6 cm) and $3^1/4$ x $4^7/8$ inches (8.3 x 12.4 cm); or use transparency film, available by the sheet at a photocopy shop; if the size of your inlay is different, adjust the size of the film as necessary

18 dollhouse nails (available at craft stores)

Large piece of charcoal or other sturdy paper, cut as described below, for the piggyback book's paper cover

SUPPLIES AND TOOLS

2 pieces of sandpaper, 125- and 220-grit, cut to fit the sanding block

Sanding block

Damp cloth for cleanup

Hand drill, or craft drill with $5/64$-inch (2 mm) drill bit, or a bit that is just slightly larger than your needle's diameter

Coping saw

Small hammer

45° triangle

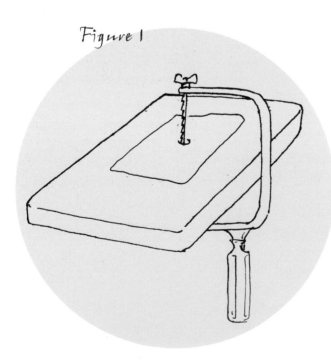

Figure 1

1 With the 125-grit sandpaper, sand the boards' corners so they are slightly rounded and won't wear through the cover material. Sand them again with the 220-grit paper, then wipe off the sawdust with a damp cloth.

2 Measure and mark a 5 x 3-inch (12.7 x 7.6 cm) window in the front cover. Cut the opening out of the wood by first drilling a hole in the middle of the area you marked, then make the opening with the coping saw (see figure 1). Sand the cuts lightly so the edges are smooth.

3 Cover both sides of the boards with torn, crumpled pieces of brown kraft paper, as described for the Gardener's Journal, step 4, on page 74.

4 Mark and cut a window for the back cover, as you did for the cover in step 2. If you use veneer for the liners, use yellow glue to adhere the two 8 x 11-inch (20.3 x 27.9 cm) pieces of veneer to the insides of the cover boards. Dry under heavy weights.

If you line the covers with charcoal paper instead, cut out the window with a mat knife first, then glue the paper to the cover with PVA. Dry under heavy weights.

5 In the example, a piece of an old map and two pressed leaves were inlaid into the front cover under a piece of clear film. Mark a rectangular area on the cover the same size as the inlay material, then use a craft knife to cut through the cover's papery covering but not into the wood itself. Carefully peel away the paper rectangle.

6 Use a small hammer and the dollhouse nails to attach the clear film over the inlay on the front cover and also to the outside of the window in the back cover.

Figure 2

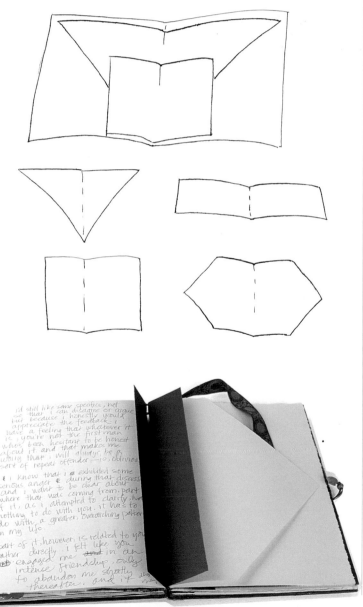

Joining the Covers to the Text Block

1 Cut some of the double text pages into interesting shapes and envelopes; several of these are shown in figure 2. Your pages can be any size and shape you like, as long as you can fold them folio-style, so they can be nested into the signature and sewn into the text block.

2 Drill the covers with a handheld drill. The text block is joined to the cover boards by a series of straight and angled holes drilled through the wood covers along the spine edges, as shown in figures 3a-c. Here, the pattern of holes forms the words *East* on one cover and *West* on the other.

A simpler alternative is to drill a single line of straight (not angled) holes in the cover boards, as for the Dream Journal (page 43). With this option, the sewn-in headbands can be added as a separate technique or left off altogether.

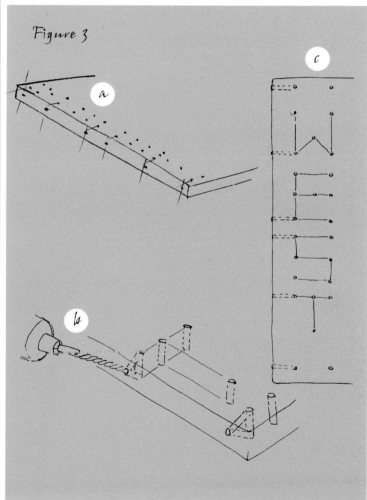

Figure 3

The stitching that creates the design in the paired holes is simply an extension of the regular stitching that joins the covers to the first and last signatures (see figure 4a). To create a stitched design this way, use an in-and-out pamphlet stitch, as shown in figure 4b.

3 Sew the covers and signatures together, following the instructions for Two-Needle Coptic binding on page 33. In this journal, the headbands are a continuation of the binding, not a separate technique. Once you add the second cover board on top of the last signature, use the needles at the head and tail to create sewn-in headbands (see Sewn-in Coptic Headbands on page 34).

Making the Piggyback Book

1 Open the map to a middle fold. Measure and mark three evenly spaced holes, then use the awl to pierce the three holes through it. Repeat this step for one of the piggyback book's accordion folds.

2 Referring to figure 5, butt the map's fold against the outside of the accordion fold, then sew them together with a three-hole pamphlet stitch (see page 100), using the tapestry needle and a length of the linen thread.

3 For the paper cover, measure the height, width, and thickness of the accordion-folded paper. Add 4 inches to the height and width measurements to allow for a 2-inch (5.1 cm) turn-in on all sides. Refer to Making the Paper Case on page 66, for instructions on how to score, cut, and fold the cover.

4 With the dollhouse nails, tack a woven ribbon over the inside cover window and up the cover, so it holds the piggyback book in its niche and also acts as a bookmark.

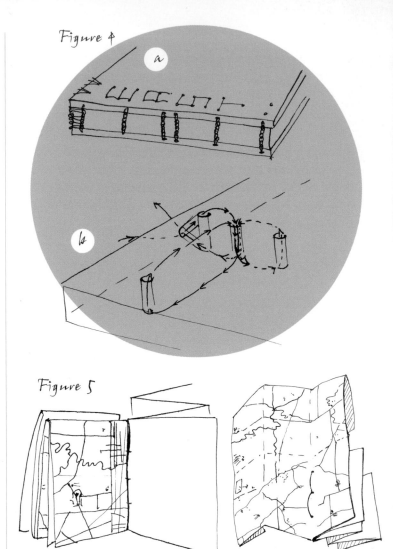

Figure 4

Figure 5

Designer:
Catharine Sutherland

Journaler:
Claire Sheldon

Designer's and Journaler's Statements:
We had a blast picking out papers, covers, the binding, and making color photocopies. It was a lot of fun putting our heads together to come up with ideas for the perfect summer journal.

CHILD'S SUMMER JOURNAL

This journal was made at a full-service photocopy shop. Most shops like these carry all the basic materials (papers, binders) and tools (scissors, glue stick) that you'll need. After going over some ideas, Catharine and Claire scoured Claire's house and bedroom for things to include in it, then headed for the shop.

BRAINSTORM FIRST!

In order to decide what type of journal you'd like to create, first ask yourself these basic questions: What do you plan to use the journal for (writing, drawing, collecting stickers, remembering a vacation)?

What size journal would best fit your needs: Do you want it to fit in your pocket or your backpack?

Will you need big pages for drawing?

Would you like the journal to have any special features, such as pockets for colored pencils, or tracing paper?

How many pages do you want it to have? What kind of paper appeals to you?

Youth is happy because it has the ability to see beauty. Anyone who keeps the ability to see beauty never grows old.

—Franz Kafka

My friends and me on Halloween. Left to right: Kaitlin, Jessica, Becky, me (Claire)

1 Once you have an idea of
the kind of journal you want to make, look for items you might like to include in the construction of the journal. Examples might be favorite photos of yourself, friends, and family; special keepsakes that could be photocopied or bound in the journal (an award certificate, a blue ribbon from a horse show, a bracelet shared with a best friend); or colorful, one-of-a-kind drawings to reproduce on a color photocopier. Assemble the items in a bag or box and head to the copy shop. You can also make interesting page inserts from a single sheet of paper (see figure 1 for ideas). Many shops provide scissors and glue sticks for you to use, or you can make the inserts ahead of time and take them with you to the shop. These can be bound in between the regular pages, so make sure they are lined up at the left edge with the rest of the papers.

2 When you arrive at the copy
shop, spend some time exploring the different types of paper available. Choose colors of paper that you like, and decide what size and weight will work best for your journal. Claire wanted a bright color scheme to go with her theme of a summer journal: she selected papers in neon green, bright orange, yellow, and white. She also picked papers from the specialty section—fun designs on invitations and printed stationery make great custom pages. Pick out as many pieces of paper as you need to make the number of pages you want. For this journal, we selected 8$\frac{1}{2}$ x 11-inch (21.6 x 27.9 cm) paper, then asked the shop to cut it in half, thus doubling the number of pages. Not all of the pages must be the same size, as long as at least part of one edge is caught by the binding.

As a special feature for this summer journal, we chose envelopes from the stationery section to include as "pouches." Claire used the pouches to hold different things, from her lemonade-stand earnings to jotted ideas for future short stories. These were bound in with the regular text pages.

3 Choose a binding style for your journal. Ask to see
which binders the copy shop offers, and pick the one that suits you best. Binders come in paper, metal,

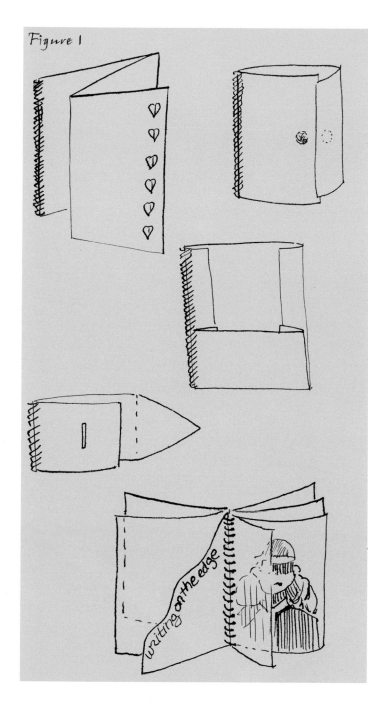

Figure 1

plastic spiral binding for this journal, because the color was the closest match to the journal's light, summery theme, and it lets the book lie flat when it's open.

4 Along with selecting a binding style, choose a cover. The shop may offer an assortment of plastic covers and card stock in different colors, or bring your own special cover material, such as decorative paper from a craft or art supply store, wrapped around card stock (see Covering Corners, on page 27, for help with covering boards). Use your imagination for ways to transform a clear or colored cover with stickers, collage, glitter, paint pens, and permanent markers. At the craft store, there are lots of fancy-edge scissors and paper punches in fun shapes, too. It's all up to you! Claire chose a clear cover, to show off the color photocopy of a favorite drawing underneath it.

5 Make use of the color and black-and-white photocopiers. If you have photographs and drawings that you want to include in your journal, use the color copier to reproduce them. This way, the originals can go back in the photo album, picture frame, or on the refrigerator. You can also make interesting images with the black-and-white copier, even if the originals are in color. Experiment with different sizes, too—reduce or enlarge the pictures to fit the style of your journal. Be sure to allow space for a margin at the left edge because the binding takes up extra space.

6 Finally, organize the pages in their proper order. Make sure they are turned in the right direction and that the edges are even before you take it to the counter to have it bound. Hand over your pages to the copy shop assistant to have them assembled with the binding you selected earlier.

and plastic, although the color selection may be limited. Remember to consider whether you want the journal to lie flat when it's open (if so, a coil binding will be best); how many pages you plan to have (pick a style that will be able to hold as many or as few as you like); and whether or not you want to be able to reopen the binding to add new pages and items to the journal. We chose a white

The written word remains. The spoken word takes wing and cannot be recalled.

— Horace

Designer:
Coral Jensen

HOLLOW BACK SPINE JOURNAL

People who love to write in blank books often want an everyday journal. This basic blank book has a comfortable shape and size, and the book cloth hinge is generous enough to allow the cover to fold well out of the way for easy writing. Designer Coral Jensen devised an ingenious alternative to sewing on tapes without using a sewing frame. When you coordinate your book cloth, cover paper, and endpapers, the journaling experience will be more inviting when you sit down to write.

FOR THE TEXT BLOCK

36 pieces of text-weight paper), cut to 6 x 12-inch (15.2 x 30.5 cm) double text pages, folded into 12 signatures

2 pieces of decorative paper, cut to 6 x 11 inches (15.2 x 27.9 cm) double text pages, folded into single-sheet folios, for the endpapers

FOR THE COVER

90 lb. (40.9 kg) watercolor paper, cut to $2^{1}/_{2}$ x $5^{7}/_{8}$ inches (6.4 x 14.9 cm)

Book cloth, cut to $8^{1}/_{4}$ x $3^{1}/_{8}$ (21 x 7.9 cm)

2 pieces of book board, cut to $5^{5}/_{8}$ x $6^{1}/_{4}$ inches (14.3 x 15.9 cm)

2 pieces of decorative paper, cut to $5^{5}/_{8}$ x $8^{1}/_{4}$ inches (14.3 x 21 cm)

SUPPLIES AND TOOLS

Linen tape

Headband

Lightweight hammer with a large, flat head

Two hardwood boards, with one end cut to a 45° wedge-shaped edge (see figure 6)

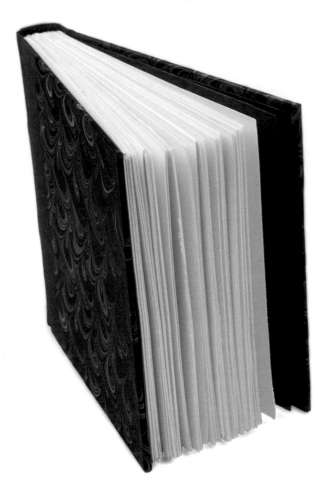

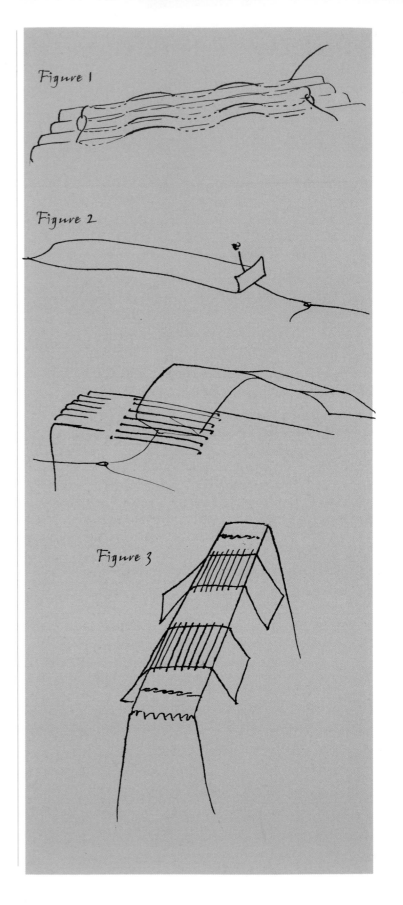

Figure 1

Figure 2

Figure 3

1 Gather your signatures together and put them under a heavy weight or in a book press until you are ready for them. Mark and pierce the signatures, as described on page 26. Begin ¼ inch (6 mm) from the head and tail, for a total of six sewing holes.

2 Thread the needle with linen thread, leaving 1 inch (2.5 cm) of thread beyond the knot. Sew the signatures together, as shown in figure 1.

Applying the Tapes

1 Set the text block between two square-edged pieces of wood, and put it into the press (or clamped) using light pressure, so that the spine extends beyond the wood. Thread a needle with 4 inches (10.2 cm) of thread and knot it. Fold over one end of one piece of linen tape, and sew a short stitch in the overlap until the knot catches in the end. Work the awl under the stitching to barely loosen the threads. Use the needle to guide the tape under these stitches (see figure 2). Cut off the knot and remove the thread from the tape. Make sure the length of tape is even

on both sides of the block. Straighten and flatten the tape so it lies flat against the spine, using the awl if necessary (see figure 3). Apply the other pieces of tape to the spine in the same way.

2 Adjust the text block in a press or between clamps, so the spine is even with the edge of the boards. With a glue brush, pound a layer of glue into the spine, so there are no gaps between the signatures, as shown in figure 4. Keep the block in the press until the glue is thoroughly dry.

3 Turn the boards so the wedge ends are on either side of the text block, one cover board–thickness below the spine, then put the block back into the press or between clamps. To round the spine, use gentle, glancing blows of the hammer from the center outward to either side (see figures 5 and 6). Be patient, and use gentle taps, working up and down the length of the spine.

4 To measure the width of the now rounded spine, lay a piece of headband against it, then cut two pieces for the head and tail. Use PVA to adhere them to the spine, as shown in figure 7.

5 Cut a $2^1/_2$ x $5^7/_8$-inch (6.4 x 14.9 cm) strip of the 90 lb. (40.9 kg) paper, and fold it into three lengthwise strips, as shown in figure 8, making sure the middle section is the exact width of the spine; the other two sections won't be quite as wide. Glue section a to section c. Adhere this piece to the spine, using the bone folder inside the hollow to firmly press it down, as in figure 9 on page 116. The hollow tube along the spine not only helps the spine keep its shape over time, but gives this method of binding its name.

Joining the Cover to the Text Block

1 Cut a piece of book cloth $8^1/_8$ x 4 inches (20.6 x 10.2 cm). Stand the spine so that it is centered on the cloth, and mark its lengthwise and crosswise positions. Now mark $^1/_4$ inch (6 mm) away from the spine marks; this leaves a space that acts like a hinge, so the cover can open wide (figure 10 on page 116).

2 Apply glue to the piece of book cloth, and lay the book board on your marks. Fold the top pieces over, onto the board. With the bone folder, burnish down the cloth to all surfaces of the board (see figure 11 on page 116).

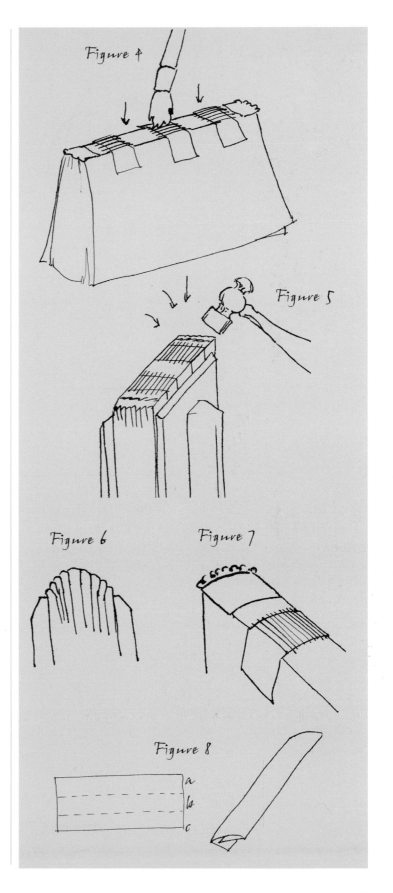

Figure 4

Figure 5

Figure 6

Figure 7

Figure 8

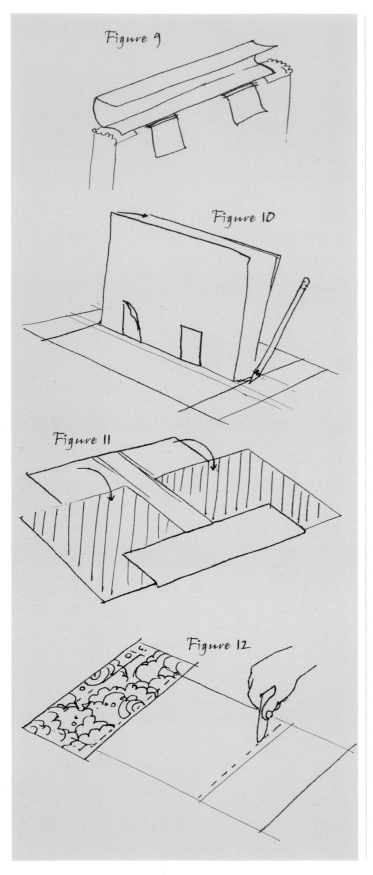

Figure 9

Figure 10

Figure 11

Figure 12

3   With the tip of the bone folder and a ruler, score a line down the book cloth ¼ inch (3 mm) in from edge; this is where you will lay the edge of the decorative paper for the cover (see figure 12).

4   Apply glue to the back of the decorative paper, and lay one edge along the scored line. Turn over the book, and cover the corners as described in the section on covering boards, page 27, using the method most appropriate for the weight of your cover material (figure 13). Repeat for the other cover.

5   Apply glue to the inside spine area of the book cloth, stand the spine in the glued area, and adhere the ends of the tapes to the book cloth and the board. Burnish down the tapes, so there are no gaps between them and the cloth and board. See figure 14. Lay wax paper between the cover and the block, and lay the book down. Gently open the cover by lifting its edge; it should overlap the block by approximately ⅛ inch (3 mm). Put the book in the press or under heavy weight, overnight. Be sure to let the spine extend beyond the press or boards, so it holds its shape.

6   Adhere the endpaper to the first sheet of the text block, as shown in figure 15.

7   Lay a piece of wax paper between the leaves of the endpaper. Apply glue to the leaf that's face up (see figure 16), then fold down the cover onto the glued paper. Open the cover and burnish down the endpaper to the inside of the cover. Repeat steps 6 and 7 to glue the other endpaper in the same way.

8   Wrap the covers, inside and out, with wax paper. Put the book under weights or in a press until thoroughly dry, making sure the spine extends beyond the press or boards.

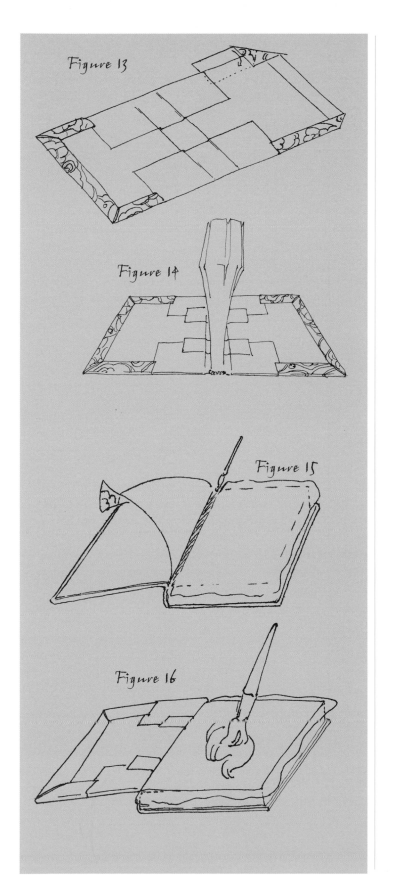

Figure 13

Figure 14

Figure 15

Figure 16

Designer:
Gwen Diehn

Although most monks' girdle books were made of leather, when other people commissioned these books, they were often made of beautiful cloth. Very few girdle books are left today. It's believed that the extension of leather on many girdle books was cut off and used for other purposes; hence the paucity of examples in existence today.

GIRDLE BOOK

This hands-free girdle book design dates from the Middle Ages, when it was primarily used by monks as a convenient way to carry their prayer books. The binding of a girdle book extends well beyond one edge of the book and, tied in a knot, can be slipped beneath your belt. Because of its small size, this lightweight volume will be available whenever and wherever you're inspired to write— it's designed to be used while still at your waist!

FOR THE TEXT BLOCK

35 sheets of smooth drawing paper, cut to 4 x 7-inch (10.2 x 17.8 cm) double text pages; folded into 7 signatures

2 sheets of decorative end-papers, cut to 4 x 7-inch (10.2 x 17.8 cm) double text pages, folded into 2 single-sheet folios (another 2 sheets, for extra endpapers, is optional; see step 8)

3 pieces of bookbinder's tape, each 3 inches (7.6 cm) long

Two-ply bookbinder's thread

Book cloth, cut to 5 x 3 inches (12.7 x 7.6 cm), for the hinge

2 pieces of headband, cut to the width of the sewn spine of the text block

FOR THE COVER

Soft, supple leather, cut to three times the width and three times the height of the sewn text block

SUPPLIES AND TOOLS

Permanent brown marker or brown shoe dye and a clean cotton rag

Decorative button

The lyf so short, the craft so long to lerne. —Chaucer

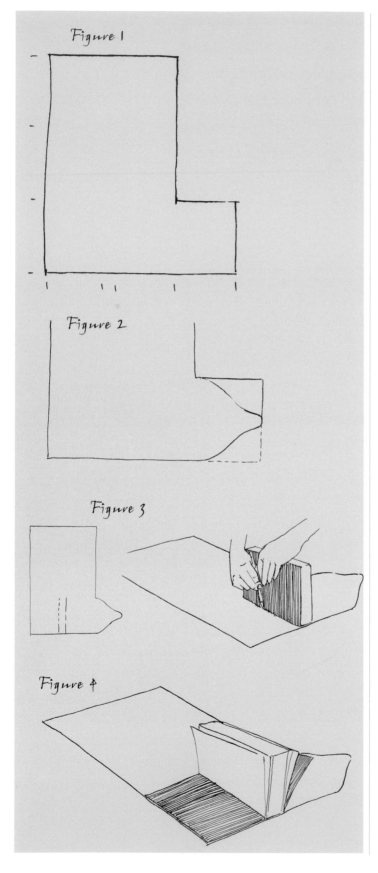

Figure 1

Figure 2

Figure 3

Figure 4

1 Fold the text papers into folios; see Folding Folios and Making Signatures on page 25.

2 Join the signatures with the tape sewing technique described on page 29.

3 Use the glue brush to pound glue into the spine of the text block.

4 Follow the steps for assembling the text block on page 30.

5 Cut out the leather in the shape shown in figure 1.

6 Trim the closing flap by first drawing one edge and cutting it with scissors. Use the piece you cut off as a pattern for cutting the second corner (see figure 2).

7 Use a permanent brown marker (or leather dye and a cloth) to color all raw edges of the leather piece.

Joining the Cover to the Text Block

1 The text block must be glued in upside down so that when the book is lifted up to write in or read from it is right side up. Therefore, turn the text block upside down, and place the spine of the text block so that the back end paper will line up with the left hand edge of the leather, about ½ inch (1.3 cm) inside the edge. Mark the placement of the spine with a pencil (see figure 3).

2 Put a piece of scrap paper between the folio pages of the back endpaper, and brush glue all over the outside sheet.

3 Remove the scrap paper. Line the spine up between the marks you made on the leather. Hold up the text block with its spine flat against the leather (see figure 4). Press the back endpaper down, and burnish it to the leather.

4 Carefully close the book so the front endpaper is on top. Repeat steps 6 and 7 for this side. Lay waxed paper between the covers and the endpapers, then press the book under a heavy weight until dry.

5 The girdle book is fastened to the wearer's belt by means of a knot or knob at the end of the cover extension. Fold in the raw edges of the leather and, if you are using very soft, supple leather, simply tie an overhand knot at the end of the extension. If you are using leather that is too stiff to tie easily, tuck the top end of the

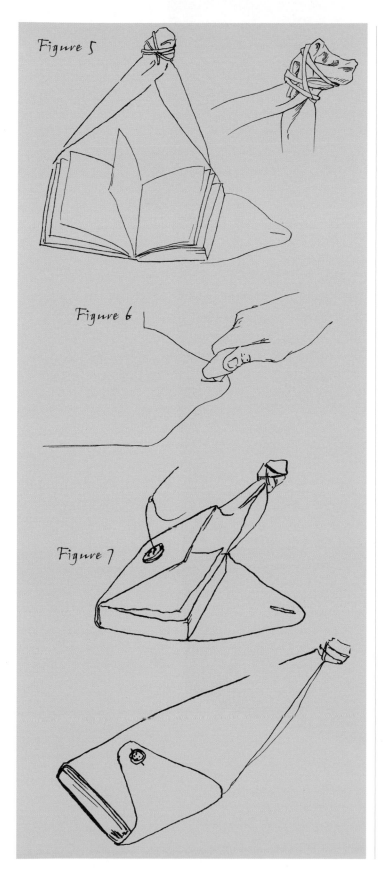

Figure 5

Figure 6

Figure 7

leather into a smooth bundle, and wrap it tightly with a strip of scrap leather, as in figure 5. Tuck the ends under the strip.

6 Close the book. Mark a place on the left cover flap for a buttonhole. Cut the buttonhole with a mat knife in the right cover extension (see figure 6).

7 Sew a button to the outside of the back of the book so it fits into the buttonhole (figure 7).

8 Glue a second set of endpapers over the first set if you want to hide the button's thread .

Nostradamus-The End of the Century Scrapbook; 1999; Ksenia Kopystynska. 20½ x 14¼ x 3 inches (52 x 36 x 7.5 cm); leather (cowhide) and handmade paper, deckle edges, antique leather, etching; photo by Contanasiuk

ACKNOWLEDGMENTS

It's been a joy for me to talk and work with the many truly creative and enthusiastic collaborators who helped bring this book to fruition. I am indebted to the four book artists whose deep love of bookmaking moves them to invest so much of themselves in their craft: Gwen Diehn, Daniel Essig, Benares Finan-Eshelman, and Coral Jensen. Thanks also to Catharine Sutherland and nine-year-old Claire Sheldon, young women whose spontaneity contributed much to their collaborative effort on Claire's Summer Journal. I am especially grateful to the 13 journalers who so generously agreed to open the pages of their journals and share their personal entries with us for this project: Amy Cook, Phil Diehn, Gwen Diehn, Priscilla Johnson, Wonder Koch, Susan Katz, Kate Mathews, Suzanne Nicaud, Bobbe Needham, Candace Stoumen, Catharine Sutherland, and Ann Turkle.

Many other people helped to make this book not only possible, but accurate and on-target. Thanks to Dorothy Africa, Keith Smith, and Roberta Lavadour for their expertise; and to ever-helpful Gwen Diehn, for her calm technical assistance at crucial intervals. Our thanks also to True Blue Art Supply and Earth Guild, both of Asheville, North Carolina, for their generosity during photo shoots.

Ocean Deep; 1999; Ksenia
Kopystynska; 21¾ x 9 x 1¾
inches (55 x 23 x 4.5 cm);
leather and handmade paper,
deckle edges, goat skin, eel skin,
flexible binding on decorative
hempcords, surface decoration
of eel skin painted with metallic
acrylic paint; photo by
Contanasiuk

DESIGNERS

Gwen Diehn teaches in the Art Department at Warren Wilson College in Swannanoa, North Carolina. She is the author of *Making Books that Fly, Fold, Wrap, Hide, Pop-Up, Twist & Turn* (Lark Books) and has nationally exhibited her drawings, prints, and artist's books.

Benares Finan-Eshelman is a core student at Penland School of Crafts, Penland, North Carolina, where she works primarily in textiles and the book arts.

Daniel Essig lives in Asheville, North Carolina, where he is a full-time studio artist specializing in the book arts, at Grovewood Studios. He earned a B.A. in Photography from Southern Illinois University at Carbondale, and often can be found at the Penland School of Crafts—as student, visiting artist, and instructor.

Coral Jensen has a Master of Fine Arts degree in Printmaking from the University of New Mexico. Originally from El Paso, Texas, Coral has one grown daughter. She began making books just a few years ago, and is the co-owner of True Blue Art Supplies in Asheville, North Carolina, and ARTPAPER.com., a retailer of fine papers for artists.

JOURNALERS

Amy Cook is a publicist in San Francisco.

Phil Diehn is a mechanical engineer who paints and writes poetry in his spare time.

Patricia Johnson does her gardening at Penland School of Crafts in North Carolina.

Susan Katz is a graphic designer and artist.

Wonder Koch creates sculpture from found objects.

Suzanne Nicaud is a book editor and author.

Kate Mathews operates a folk/ethnic clothing pattern business.

Bobbe Needham is a freelance editor.

Claire Sheldon is a budding writer and artist.

Candace Stoumen is a mother who works, writes, paints, and dreams in the mountains of Vermont.

Catharine Sutherland teaches yoga.

Ann Turkle teaches writing and poetry.

GALLERY CONTRIBUTORS

Elizabeth Clark, (page 6) Mussaku, Phoenix, Arizona

Mary Crest, (pages 13, 17) Pomona, California

Sheila Cunningham, (page 16) Richardson, Texas

Wendy Hale Davis, (pages 7, 8, 14) Austin, Texas

Stephanie Dean-Moore, (page 15) Nova Scotia, Canada

Ksenia Kopystynska, (pages 11, 122, 124) Ars Libri Studio, Edmonton, Alberta, Canada

Roberta Lavadour, (page 16-17) Pendleton, Oregon

Claudia Lee, (pages 11, 14) Smithville, Tennessee

Emily Martin, (page 13) Iowa City, Iowa

Andrea A. Peterson, (pages 12, 15) Laporte, Indiana

Pamela Lyle Westhaver/Papers by Pam, (pages 10, 16) Prince George, British Columbia, Canada

GLOSSARY *of Journal Making Terms*

Archival. A general term used to indicate an acid-free material. Often used interchangeably with pH neutral.

Awl. Tool used for piercing holes.

Bond. A lightweight, general-purpose paper; usually weighs 12 to 20 lbs. (5.4 to 9.1 kg) per ream

Bone folder. Tool, made of bone or plastic, used to obtain crisp folds and to burnish glued materials.

Book press. Cast iron device used to apply varying degrees of pressure to a just-glued book.

Bookbinder's board. Rigid, dense, gray paperboard; used to make covers.

Book cloth. Closely woven fabric, usually sized, that is thin and flexible; used to cover boards and to act as a hinge between the spine and cover boards

Bradawl. Same as awl.

Burnish. Tool used to apply smooth pressure to just-glued materials, in order to achieve a firm bond.

Cover board. Material used to create rigid, protective encasement for the text block.

Cradle. V-shaped trough, used to hold an opened signature while the sewing holes are made.

Deckle edge. The rough edge of a handmade paper.

Double text page. A sheet of paper cut to twice the individual page size.

Eggbeater drill. Hand tool used to pierce holes in heavier materials, such as bookbinder's board and wood.

Endpaper. Protective folio, often of decorative paper, adhered to the first and last sheets of the text block. When it is not printed, it is also known as a flyleaf.

Folio. A single sheet of paper folded exactly in half.

Flyleaf. A blank sheet or sheets at the beginning or end of a book.

Fore edge. The end of the book that is on the side opposite the spine.

Glue brush. A coarse-bristled, round brush used to apply adhesive.

Glue tab. When covering boards, the extra material that will be wrapped around and adhered to the edges and part of the inside surface of a cover board.

Grain. The predominant direction of the longer plant fibers in a sheet of paper; runs either along the length or the width of the sheet.

Head. When the spine is to the left, the top edge of the book.

Headband. Thread sewn over cord and cloth; used at the head and tail of the text block, where the signatures are joined.

Hole punch. Any one of several machined metal tools used to create small, clean-edged openings in various materials.

Laminate. To adhere two similar materials, such as paper or wood, that are exactly the same size.

Linen tape. Woven, nonadhesive ribbon used to give greater support to a sewn gathering of signatures.

Needle awl. Pointed tool used to make holes.

Paired stations. In Coptic binding, two lines of side-by-side sewing holes that cross the width of the text block's spine, and are stitched with two needles on a single length of thread.

Perfect binding. Single sheets glued together at the left edges to create the text block.

pH neutral. On a scale of 0 to 14, an indication of the midpoint between the acidity and alkalinity of a material.

PVA. An adhesive made with polyvinyl acetate, often referred to as craft glue.

Ream. A term used by paper manufacturers to indicate 500 sheets of paper.

Signature. Sheets of paper folded and gathered to form more than one page; folios are nested inside one another, but a quarto (a two-fold sheet) is itself a signature.

Sizing. A glutinous material used as filler for paper or cloth.

Skiving. A shaving technique, used to reduce the thickness of leather; used with a skiver tool.

Spine stiffener. A woven or paper material adhered to the spine of the text block to give it greater support.

Spine. When the book faces up, the left edge from head to tail.

Square knot. A secure, left-over-right, then right-over-left, tying of two threads.

Station. A line of sewing holes that extends across the width of the text block's spine.

Stitching awl. A hand tool that simultaneously pierces and sews a line of stitches; the thread is held in a bobbin.

TAIL. When the spine is to the left, the bottom edge of the book.

Tapestry needle. A blunt-ended needle with a large eye.

Text weight. A lightweight paper suitable for writing.

Text block. A gathering of signatures.

Turn-in. When covering, the extra material that will be wrapped around and adhered to the edges and inside surface of a cover board.

Upholstery needle. Curved needle with a large eye; used with heavier thread.

Weaver's knot. A flat knot used to join a new length of thread to the old one.

Wet tear. Tearing technique used to simulate a deckle edge on a piece of paper.

INDEX